TRANSGENDER HEALTH

of related interest

Gender Diversity and Non-Binary Inclusion in the Workplace
The Essential Guide for Employers
Sarah Gibson and J. Fernandez
ISBN 978 1 78592 244 2
eISBN 978 1 78450 523 3

Counseling Transgender and Non-Binary Youth
The Essential Guide
Irwin Krieger
ISBN 978 1 78592 743 0
eISBN 978 1 78450 482 3

The Voice Book for Trans and Non-Binary People
A Practical Guide to Creating and Sustaining Authentic Voice and Communication
Matthew Mills and Gillie Stoneham
ISBN 978 1 78592 128 5
eISBN 978 1 78450 394 9

Transgender Employees in the Workplace
A Guide for Employers
Jennie Kermode
ISBN 978 1 78592 228 2
eISBN 978 1 78450 544 8

Trans Voices
Becoming Who You Are
Declan Henry
Foreword by Professor Stephen Whittle, OBE
Afterword by Jane Fae
ISBN 978 1 78592 240 4
eISBN 978 1 78450 520 2

TRANSGENDER HEALTH

A Practitioner's Guide to Binary and Non-Binary Trans Patient Care

BEN VINCENT, PhD

Foreword by Dr Stuart Lorimer

Jessica Kingsley *Publishers*
London and Philadelphia

First published in 2018
by Jessica Kingsley Publishers
73 Collier Street
London N1 9BE, UK
and
400 Market Street, Suite 400
Philadelphia, PA 19106, USA

www.jkp.com

Library of Congress Cataloging in Publication Data
A CIP catalog record for this book is available from the Library of Congress

British Library Cataloguing in Publication Data
A CIP catalogue record for this book is available from the British Library

ISBN 978 1 78592 201 5
eISBN 978 1 78450 475 5

Printed and bound in Great Britain

To Kine

Contents

Foreword

Dr Stuart Lorimer

Who treats gender dysphoria? At the time of writing, this varies throughout the UK. For reasons largely historical, the majority of care for binary and non-binary trans people happens within Gender Identity Clinics staffed by a mixture of clinicians but, in theory at least, any doctor including the GP can initiate and manage hormones.

Who *should* treat gender dysphoria? This is perhaps a knottier issue. In 2016, the House of Commons Women and Equalities Select Committee released its report on Transgender Equality, noting with concern the continued bracketing of gender within the realm of mental health, and suggesting this gave the misleading impression of trans status being a "disorder of the mind". It recommended transferring gender services to another area of clinical specialism or viewing them as "a distinct specialism in their own right".

I came into this field in 2002 as a consultant in general adult and liaison psychiatry. At that time, gender clinics were the near-exclusive province of psychiatrists. Within a year or two, however, the professional landscape was changing, with psychologists, endo-crinologists and even the occasional oncologist joining the fray.

This is as it should be. While I believe that liaison psychiatry provides a good skill-set for approaching the topic, gender-related issues can and do arise in all areas of medicine, most commonly in primary care.

With greater mainstream discussion – and, for the most part, acceptance – trans individuals become aware of their options and present earlier, typically to the GP.

The aforementioned Select Committee report pointed out that GPs, "too often lack an understanding of: trans identities; the diagnosis of gender dysphoria...and their own role in prescribing hormone treatment".

It is understandable that a GP faced with their first transgender patient might feel out of their depth, trans people and their healthcare having tended to be a mere footnote in medical education. Recalling my own training, it wasn't until my Royal College of Psychiatrists membership exam in the late 1990s that "transsexualism" merited more than the briefest of mentions.

In 2014, I visited the adult gender service clinic in Toronto, run by consultant psychiatrist Dr Chris McIntosh. The set-up felt simultaneously familiar and unfamiliar. One significant difference was that those arriving at the Toronto clinic from all over Ontario were already established on a hormone regimen; Dr McIntosh and his colleagues focused predominantly on assessing people's eligibility and readiness for gender-related surgery.

Had the Toronto cohort self-medicated? No, they were all started on hormones by local services, which then carried out blood testing and adjusted dosage as needed, seemingly without undue difficulty. I wondered whether this related in part to the fact that many Canadian cities have a medical practice located within the LGBT neighbourhood and, over time, clinicians at those practices had become sufficiently experienced to prescribe and monitor with confidence.

In terms of similarly LGBT-experienced UK establishments, we have the fantastic cliniQ in London and Brighton's Clinic T, both of which do an excellent job.

The Toronto model went further, though, with what seemed a more formalised hub-and-spoke relationship between the central gender clinic and further-flung general practices. Where issues arose that couldn't be handled at a local level, the main clinic was well-placed to advise.

This seems, ultimately, the way ahead for gender care. Demand is increasing on a global scale due to increasing awareness and, happily, acceptance. We, as a profession, no longer have the luxury of treating trans as an esoteric little micro-speciality. Trans is defiantly mainstream.

In this book, Ben Vincent aims to bridge the gap between perceived specialism and everyday healthcare. This is not an abstruse academic textbook, relevant to a select few; it is a meticulously researched "how to" guide that addresses every commonplace circumstance encountered in gender healthcare, from appropriate terminology and pronoun etiquette (including how to manage the situation of not knowing the correct pronouns) to the nuts and bolts of hormone management.

This book is truly democratic and, above all, *practical.* Trans healthcare belongs to all of us and it is the duty of every medical practitioner to manage gender-related issues safely and effectively. This book is a vital and timely step toward that.

Dr Stuart Lorimer is a consultant psychiatrist and senior gender specialist at the NHS gender identity clinic at Charing Cross Hospital, where he has worked since 2002 and been directly involved in the face-to- face assessment and care of an estimated four thousand people with gender issues. He is a member of the Royal College of Psychiatrists, WPATH, EPATH and BAGIS and is listed on the HM Government Gender Recognition Panel's list of specialists in the field of gender dysphoria. Pronouns: he/him/his.

Acknowledgements

My thanks to Emma Holak, Andrew James, Jessica Kingsley, Sammy Patrick, and Daisy Watt at Jessica Kingsley Publishers for the final stages of bringing this book to press. I am enormously grateful to Bernard and Terry Reed, not only for their decades of trans activism and the warmth of their friendship, but for their belief and support of my work. I have been privileged to draw upon a wealth of experience and expertise from many wonderful trans people. Huge thanks go to Jess Bradley, Alex Brett, Jamie Fletcher, Sam Hope, Samuel Heyes, Emma-Ben Lewis, Kate Hutchinson, CN Lester, James Morton, Jude Taylor, and Reubs Walsh. My thanks to Jos Twist, Tanner Gibbins-Klein, and Stuart Lorimer for their extremely diligent review of the manuscript, catching and clarifying all sorts of points which I otherwise would have missed. Thanks also to John Wilkinson for feedback from a GP's perspective, and Leighton Seal for his endocrinological expertise. I am also deeply grateful to Stuart Lorimer for his contribution of the foreword for this book – his professional expertise and approach to trans healthcare is reflected by his stellar reputation in the trans community. Special thanks especially go to my inspirational friends and colleagues Ruth Pearce, Michael Toze, and Allison Washington, who have given more time and energy in offering suggestions and proofreading of the final manuscript than I could have hoped for. Thanks also to my mum, Sally Vincent, who generously shared her home with Kine and me when much of this book was written (during the post-PhD, pre-employment limbo!) Finally, gratitude always to Kine, for putting up with all my doggo ways.

Chapter 1

Introducing Trans Terminology

Transgender healthcare spans a wide range of services providing for the care of transgender people, whose needs can be widely different, and occasionally contradictory. This scope presents a challenge in education and methods for those who would serve these needs, and for those who require those services. This book provides a comprehensive resource for addressing those challenges.

Whether you are a student or an experienced practitioner seeking to expand your knowledge and understanding, part of a patient-practitioner liaison or training programme, or are yourself trans and looking for information to assist you in your navigation of the healthcare system, you should find what you're looking for here.

This book presents its discussions differently to earlier literature on transgender health. Most of the existing literature has only considered gender transition, where an individual seeks to access hormones and/or surgeries to affirm the gender they identify with. This is, of course, a central theme of this book; however, it is also important to consider the treatment of trans patients in cases where their trans status is indirectly relevant or not relevant at all. Earlier work has tended to focus on the biomechanical aspects of medicine, including aetiology (theories of causation), and differing surgical techniques. Again, such factors will be discussed, but with shifts in emphasis to recognise limitations and critiques of the former, and using more sensitive, modern language.

It is important that the service user feels they are taken seriously, respected, understood, and safe. A familiarity with how to approach language is crucial – as using outdated terms or failing to respect a patient's name and title may result in loss of trust, damaging the provider-client relationship. Here then is the terminology currently in use and generally considered appropriate and respectful. It is important to note that language changes over time, and so as this book ages, readers should be mindful that language preferences may have changed since this book was published in 2018.

Transgender (usually shortened to 'trans') is used to describe people whose felt sense of gender – their gender identity – is not the same as the gender assumed at birth on the basis of genital appearance[1]. This phrasing is important – saying 'born a boy/girl' should be avoided, as this centralises one aspect of sex/gender (the genitals) over all others. Being *labelled* male or female (or, in some cases, intersex) is done at birth, by a cursory glance at the genitals. However, this does not tell us how the infant will necessarily relate to gender in the future. Nor does this accurately determine an individual's chromosomes or gonads, the secondary sexual characteristics they will later develop, or what hormone levels will be produced.

Rather than sex being a binary of male/female, we can better understand human biology as bimodal – having two large majorities, but with many other variations possible. Whilst most babies assigned male will also have testes, XY chromosomes, and later experience a masculinising puberty, we know this is not true for all, even among those people born with penises who also identify as men. This highlights some of the assumptions that are made from genitalia alone. In day-to-day life, gender is routinely judged from appearance, and inferences made about bodies on this basis (for example, someone perceived to be 'a woman' is assumed to have breasts, a vagina, vulva, XX chromosomes, etc.). Kessler and McKenna (1978) called this process the 'cultural genitals', showing how the supposed 'neutral' or 'natural' facts of sex have enormous interplay with the social world.

Most people will grow up feeling that the gender assumed at birth reflects their sense of self, and thus are **cisgender** (which

---

1   Chapter 2 goes into detail about the fundamental categories of sex and gender, and how these terms are used.

can be shortened to 'cis'[2]). The word cisgender simply tells us about a person's relationship with their assignment at birth, just like the word transgender does. Many people fail to realise that when saying 'man' and 'woman', this can mean cis and/or trans people. 'Cis' does the same work as 'heterosexual'. When the term heterosexuality was first introduced in 1886[3] (later than the term 'homosexual', first used in 1869 by Karl-Maria Kertbeny), it too was defined as a pathology. According to the 1901 Dorland's Medical Dictionary, heterosexuality was an 'abnormal or perverted appetite toward the opposite sex', only coming to mean 'normal' sexual orientation years later (Katz 2007). As soon as more than one sexual orientation was acknowledged to exist, a term was needed for the majority group. Before that, the 'normal category' went unnamed. Everyone was assumed to be 'normal', that is, to have sexual appetites for the opposite sex, until proven otherwise. This made it easy for anyone who was not part of the majority to be (troublingly) positioned as 'abnormal'. How homosexuality and transsexuality were conceived as 'sicknesses' is linked to this silent default (this is covered in Chapter 2).

The link between sexual orientation and gender identity should not result in confusion, as these are distinctly different. Put simply, sexual orientation concerns who one wishes to go to bed *with*, whilst gender identity is who one goes to bed *as*. Clinicians should only ask questions about a trans person's sexual orientation if the context is one in which they would also need to ask about a cis person's sexual orientation. It is, however, useful to understand how labels of sexuality may be deployed in the particular context of trans people. Consider a trans woman (someone who was assigned male at birth and who identifies as a woman): if she is exclusively attracted to men, her status as a woman means she is straight. If she is exclusively attracted to women, her status as a woman makes her a lesbian. She could also be bisexual, or describe her sexuality in another way, such as queer (see later in this chapter) or asexual. Sexuality labels depend upon the individual's *gender* as a point of reference, and one should always take the person's gender identity, *not* the birth assignment, as the point of reference.

---

2   Pronounced 'sis'.
3   By Richard von Krafft-Ebing, in his book *Psychopathia Sexualis*.

The title of this book may have raised a question: what does it mean to demarcate trans people's identities as 'binary' or 'non-binary'? The **gender binary** is the system whereby all individuals are classified into one of two – and only two – gender categories: man, and woman. The existence of intersex individuals demonstrates this as an over-simplification of biological variation, and the same complexity can be seen in people's gender identities.[4] Trans men (people assigned female at birth who identify as men) and trans women (people assigned male at birth who identify as women) are examples of **binary** (-oriented) identities. Whilst not identifying with the sex/gender assigned at birth, they still fit within the gender binary. **Non-binary** trans people identify as neither men nor women. Many examples of other genders have existed throughout history, and across different cultures (Herdt 1993) as well as in present day Western contexts (Richards *et al.* 2017). Non-binary is used as an umbrella term, as it covers many different experiences and labels of gender. This is detailed in the glossary below.

Terminology is constantly evolving, and it is important to recognise that different words can have different meanings for different people. A term may adequately describe one person's affirmed identity, whilst simultaneously being horribly insulting to someone else, thus creating a potentially difficult linguistic landscape for the service provider. The following glossary therefore includes wider discussions to provide deeper context, and avoid 'rote learning'. If in doubt when interacting with a trans person, it is best to learn how they wish to be addressed and how they understand themselves, on a case-by-case basis. When in doubt, ask.

As time moves on, this glossary will no doubt also become dated. However, the central theme of an open, holistic, and individualised approach is always the best practice in transgender healthcare.

---

4   It is beyond the scope of this book to give a full discussion of the relationship between bodies, culture, history, and the rich research examining these factors. However, it is important that we avoid thinking of bodies as more 'fundamentally true' than identities, as this not only fails to recognise how biology shapes identity through neurology and psychology, but also how the social world is responsible for the construction of the meaning given to biological structures. In short, we cannot separate 'biological' and 'social' factors in a way that doesn't produce an artificial hierarchy, which arbitrarily puts some factors of sex/gender over others, and ultimately creates a bias that can negatively impact patient access to care.

Glossary

Affirmed gender: a person's affirmed gender, describes the gender status achieved after transition (see below). This means that their general appearance, name and pronouns are brought into line with their gender identity (see below), thus affirming it. The term 'affirmed', may be used in preference to 'acquired' which refers, specifically, to the social gender status and legal protection bestowed when a Gender Recognition Certificate (GRC) is obtained. The term 'acquired' should be regarded as referring to the altered gender *status*, of the individual, rather than any change to their gender identity. Personal identities cannot be 'acquired'. The term 'chosen gender' should also be avoided. Note that not every trans person undergoes medical transition (or even social transition) – and so the fact that one can conceive of interventions/changes as 'affirming' should not imply that trans people who do not want/ need such things are correspondingly 'not affirmed'. Different trans people have widely differing needs in relation to their trans status – this language is simply to frame how transition works to help them feel right about their body and/or navigation of the social world, even though validity as their gender does not *depend* on any given transition process.

Assignment at birth: a phrase used to indicate how someone's sex (and, therefore, gender) was identified and registered on the birth certificate, according to observation of the genitalia. This phrasing recognises that genitals are only one signifier of sex/gender, and that for both trans and intersex people, genitals may not reflect their identities or other gendered aspects of anatomy and physiology. For example, an adult with 'male' on their birth certificate may have a vagina. This person could have been assigned female at birth but have received a Gender Recognition Certificate allowing a new birth certificate. Alternatively, they could have been assigned male at birth but have received vaginoplasty. Both of these individuals would be trans[5], yet this phrase allows us to clearly understand a patient's history without disenfranchising the validity of their identity. Assigned male at birth can be abbreviated as **AMAB**, and

---

5   Some trans people do not identify as 'trans', but may instead describe themselves as a 'person with a trans history'.

assigned female at birth can be abbreviated as **AFAB**. While AMAB and AFAB are the most common terms used, different people may prefer a variation with broadly the same meaning. Examples that some people may prefer are **DMAB/DFAB** (designated male/female at birth), and **CAMAB/CAFAB** (coercively assigned male/female at birth). Debates around this terminology intersect with intersex healthcare.

Cisgender: often shortened to 'cis', this term indicates someone whose gender matches their assignment at birth. Therefore, a cisgender woman is someone assigned female at birth (labelled 'female' based on a vulva being observed) who identifies as a woman. Conversely, a cisgender man is someone assigned male at birth, who identifies as a man. Historically, when the words 'men' and 'women' were used (without the prefix 'trans'), this would always be about cisgender men and women only, which problematically excludes trans people from being included as 'real' men or women. In short, cisgender acts as a simple modifier to indicate people who are not trans. This does not say anything about a person's relationships with masculinity, femininity, socially constructed 'gender roles', or gender expression.

Cissexism: refers to interactions, processes, and systems that position cisgender individuals as 'normal' and 'natural' and, therefore, preferable, or superior (implying that trans is 'abnormal' and 'unnatural'). A simple example would be a use of the word 'women' which excluded trans women. Cissexism results in privilege for individuals who are cisgender. Further examples of cissexism might include assuming that all people who are men have XY chromosomes, documents that have only 'male' and 'female' as options, without including 'non-binary' or permitting self-declaration, or assuming that it is reasonable to ask a trans person highly personal questions out of curiosity alone – such as about their genitalia. This puts cisgender curiosity ahead of trans comfort, when asking such questions of another cisgender person would be regarded as invasive and extremely rude.

Cross-dressing: there is a complex relationship between cross-dressing, gender identity and sexual orientation. The term literally refers to a person wearing clothing associated with the 'opposite sex', although now almost always deployed to talk about a man wearing 'women's clothing'. Note that this is a problematic phrase. When a woman purchases a shirt, or trousers, we do not refer to them as 'men's clothing' – it is understood that such an association is archaic. Clothing does not 'belong' to any given gender. Phrases such as 'women's clothing', whilst communicating meaning, subtly reinforce a rigid division between what is positioned as 'normal' gendered behaviour, and gender presentation.

The term has, for many, replaced the older word **transvestite**. Transvestism was the medical definition for sexual interest in cross-dressing (again, with almost all consideration being of people assigned male at birth). The term transvestite is now considered offensive by many; however, others still self-identify with this term, particularly older people. The vast majority of trans people (particularly trans women) are likely to be very offended if they are referred to as a transvestite or cross-dresser, as this implies that their identity is a sexual fetish, or runs no deeper than clothing choice. This is fundamentally untrue for all trans people.

Further, most drag queens (see below) do not identify as cross-dressers, and many individuals may explore a different gender presentation through cross-dressing before coming out as trans, whilst never identifying with the term cross-dresser. Be mindful that because these words hold different meanings for different people, both cis and trans, the point of being careful to remember how a person describes themselves and following their lead/assertion is advised.

Deadname: most trans people change their name, commonly as part of a social transition. A trans person's deadname is the term used for the name given in infancy. Due to the gendered nature of most names, hearing one's deadname can be distressing, and potentially trigger dysphoria (see gender dysphoria below). This is particularly relevant in the waiting room – a system that relies on staff calling out the name on a patient record may be extremely embarrassing or upsetting if the name does not match their gender presentation. Some trans people experience great anxiety over the potential of this happening and may walk out and not return, or eschew medical care altogether. Further, a trans patient does not need to seek or have accessed medical transition for their name to be changed on their patient record. There is no legal process that must be followed to start using a new name. (A full account of Deed Polls and changes to patients' records is given in Chapter 3.) Standard ethical practice should include asking a patient who is known to be trans what name and pronouns they wish to be addressed by.

Drag queen: drag queens dress in 'women's clothing' (often with a fantastical, theatrical, or exaggerated style) for the purposes of entertainment such as cabaret shows, or as an enjoyable practice long associated with the LGBTQ community. Drag queens are often assumed to be cisgender gay (or bisexual) men, however it is possible for individuals of all sexual orientations and gender identities to be drag queens. Most importantly, being a drag queen does *not* mean an individual does not identify with the gender they were assigned at birth, and therefore being a drag queen does not make an individual trans. Older definitions of 'transgender' could stretch to include all individuals who express gender non-conformity, however this has resulted in a great deal of confusion between gender *identity* and gender *expression*. Many trans people (particularly trans women) would be very insulted to be called a drag queen, as this could imply that their experience of womanhood is simply 'dressing up for fun'. However, certain trans women (or men) may also be drag queens.

Drag king: like drag queens, drag kings are often individuals assigned female at birth who engage in 'male impersonation' as a performance, LGBTQ entertainment, or community involvement. The same logic applies for drag kings as for drag queens above – being a drag king does not mean that someone is trans; however, trans people can be drag kings.

Gender affirming surgeries: some (importantly: not all) trans people require one or more surgeries to reduce or remove the experience of gender dysphoria. The phrase illustrates that rather than 'turning men into women' or vice versa, the individual's *identity* positions them as male, female, or non-binary regardless of their body. Altering the body thus affirms the person's gender identity. Surgeries can be hugely significant in the relief of distress, and make it easier to be 'read' as male or female by other people (sometimes referred to as 'passing'). This can significantly reduce an individual's risk of experiencing transphobic discrimination or violence. These are also sometimes referred to as 'gender confirmation surgeries'. They have also previously been referred to as 'sex/gender reassignment surgeries', yet this is outdated and should not be used. Within a surgical context, more specific, operationalised language is usually preferred – such as 'genital reconstructive surgery', 'chest augmentation/reconstruction surgery' or 'facial feminisation surgery'. This is because the language of gender affirmation does not adequately specify body part(s) or procedure type.

Some examples of gender affirming surgeries for trans women include vaginoplasty, breast implants, and facial feminisation procedures. For trans men, some examples include phalloplasty (construction of a penis), salpingo-oophorectomy (removal of fallopian tubes and ovaries), hysterectomy, and mastectomy. Procedures (for any gender) to the chest may be colloquially referred to as 'top surgery' and to the genitalia as 'bottom' or 'lower surgery'. Phono-surgery may be undertaken by trans women to try to raise the pitch of the voice.

Gender dysphoria: this medical term refers to the potentially immense distress that some (but not all) trans people experience as a result of the incongruence between their gender identity and assignment at birth. Some experience this strongly in relation to their bodies (physical dysphoria), and may find that only access to hormones and/or gender affirming surgeries provide relief. Gender dysphoria may also manifest because of particular social interactions (social dysphoria), such as having their gender misread because of their physical characteristics of their assignment at birth, such as height, facial bone structure, and voice. This may put pressure on those who are not otherwise uncomfortable with their bodies to seek to alter their bodies. However, decisions about such interventions not to alter their bodies include dissatisfaction with the limits of surgery, being unable to access surgeries or hormones due to other medical conditions, stigma, and pressure from other people in their lives, or finding the risks of surgery or hormones too great. Many trans people reject the simplistic understanding of trans people as all 'trapped in the wrong body', instead understanding that a trans woman who chooses not to have medical interventions still has a woman's body, due to it being a body that belongs to a woman. What it means 'to be' a gender is not defined by sexual physiology or anatomy, but by identity.

Attempts to treat gender dysphoria with therapy to 'cure' someone of being trans – i.e. alter their gender identity – are not an ethical treatment pathway and can be gravely dangerous, leading only to repression and high rates of suicidality and suicide. Such 'conversion therapy' has been condemned as abuse by The British Association for Counselling and Psychotherapy, The British Association for Behavioural and Cognitive Psychotherapies, The British Psychoanalytic Council, The British Psychological Society, The College of Sexual and Relationship Therapists, GLADD (The Association of LGBT Doctors and Dentists), The National Counselling Society, National Health Service Scotland, Pink Therapy, The Royal College of General Practitioners, The Scottish Government, Stonewall, and The UK Council for Psychotherapy.

A technical note that is also relevant here is the fact that gendered distress experienced by trans people is recognised differently in different technical manuals. While the Diagnostic and Statistical Manual of Mental disorders (DSM-5; American Psychiatric Association 2013) uses the term gender dysphoria, the International Classification of Diseases (ICD-10; World Health Organization 1992) uses the deeply problematic and out-of-date term 'transsexualism'. This is due to the latest edition of the DSM being released in 2013, but the ICD not being updated since 1990. The forthcoming new edition of the ICD is set to update to the term '**gender incongruence**'. Practitioners should recognise the difference between a medical diagnosis and a trans identity. While diagnoses are used to recognise distress needing medical intervention, no doctor can 'diagnose someone as trans'.

Gender non-conformity/gender diversity: these terms are used to refer to gender expression – that is, how masculinity and/or femininity are expressed. Someone's trans status is not dependent upon their conforming to or rejecting gender roles or norms of gender presentation. As an example, a trans man may regard himself as gender non-conforming if subverting gendered expectations by wearing make-up or jewellery. This does not make him any 'less' of a man, any more than it would if he were cisgender. Clearly then, cisgender people (by this definition) may also be gender non-conforming, however there is also an association between the terms gender non-conformity/gender diversity and non-binary gender identities. Non-binary people may conform to gendered expectations (in alignment with the gender they were assigned at birth or the other gender recognised within the gender binary) without this making them 'less non-binary', because their gender identity is separate from their gender expression. Gender diversity is also frequently used in the discussion of children who articulate discomfort with their assignment at birth, as this more broadly recognises that flexibility, exploration, and potential rejection of stereotypical gendered behaviour does not necessarily mean a trans identity will be embraced, or social/medical transition will be wanted. The term **gender variance** is sometimes used, but has been challenged for potentially implying trans people are a 'variant' from cis people in a manner that may imply 'abnormality'.

Genderqueer: a term that is roughly synonymous with non-binary identity. Genderqueer arose as an identity label somewhat earlier (approximately the early 1990s) and may also carry a connotation of a non-conforming gender expression. Genderqueer thus may carry a more political element, rejecting or challenging more normative ideas of gender roles and expression. The term 'queer' has negative connotations for some (particularly older) people, therefore care should be exercised in following the lead of how people describe themselves.

Intersex: this is an umbrella term referring to conditions where sex-differentiation is not uniformly achieved, resulting in variation in their gendered physiology and/or anatomy. The most visible manifestation of an intersex person is someone born with ambiguous genitalia – neither clearly male nor female (under the system that categorises all infants as one or the other). There is a long and troubling history of babies with such genitalia being surgically modified for cosmetic reasons only, without the informed consent of parents[6], and clearly without the consent

---

6   In 2011, Christiane Völling became the first person to successfully sue for damages for non-consensual intersex surgical intervention, being awarded €100,000 by the Regional Court of Cologne (Zwischengeschlect.org 2011).

of the child. Other examples of intersex variation include XO, XXY, or XYY chromosomal patterns (Turner's, Klinefelter's, and Jacob's syndromes, respectively), or the inability of cells to respond to androgens (Androgen Insensitivity Syndrome). Some intersex conditions may require medical intervention to maintain good health, such as Congenital Adrenal Hyperplasia, which is associated with 'salt-wasting' at the time of birth – while others do not. Some cases are symptomatically visible, while others may go unrecognised for much of, or all, of a person's life (sometimes being discovered if facing fertility issues). Intersex has come to replace the term **hermaphrodite** or **pseudo-hermaphrodite**, which many intersex people find highly offensive and archaic. The term **disorders of sex development (DSDs)** is used by some texts, policies, and practitioners. This is sometimes done synonymously with intersex, or can be to attempt to differentiate between non-pathological intersex variation and congenital conditions which require intervention. This is a highly controversial term, particularly because of its use of 'disorder' which some intersex people may dispute. Others use DSD to stand for **differences of sex development**, to avoid this stigmatisation.

A detailed consideration of intersex is beyond the scope of this book. The reason intersex is included in this glossary is chiefly to illustrate the differences with trans people, and also the potential for overlap. Many intersex people have a male or female gender identity, while some will identify specifically as intersex (instead of, or in addition to, being a man or a woman). Many intersex babies are still ultimately assigned as male or female, based on the measurement of the phallus at birth. If later they do not identify with this assignment, they may identify as trans. Being intersex does not mean one is trans, and being trans does not mean one is intersex. However, a trans person may be intersex (with or without their knowledge), and an intersex person may be trans, if they do not identify with their assignment at birth.

LGBTQ: An acronym which stands for lesbian, gay, bisexual, transgender, and queer. There is a historical association between gender and sexual minorities (**GSMs**), though more recently there has been a clearer distinction between sexual orientations and gender identities. Variations of this acronym exist to include a broader spectrum, such as **LGBT+**, **LGBTQ+**, **LGBTQIA+**,[7] etc. **GSRD** is also sometimes used for gender, sexual, and relationship diversities.

Misgendering: The use of pronouns or other descriptors (e.g., Mr/Ms, sir/ma'am) which contradict someone's gender identity. One may assume a person's gender on the basis of how they appear (due to physical traits and/or gendered appearance) and make mistakes quite unwittingly and without malicious intention. Nevertheless, this may still result in heightened dysphoria. This highlights the importance of using gender neutral language ('good morning' rather than 'good morning sir/madam', for example) unless a person's mode of address/gender identity is known.

Non-binary: A non-binary person has a gender identity that is neither (exclusively) male nor female. This contrasts with most people who identify within the gender binary – that is, as simply men, or women (whether cis or trans). Non-binary, like transgender, can be understood as an umbrella term, including a wide range of different experiences of gender and different gender identity labels. Some individuals may feel their gender is neutral, or that they do not have a gender identity at all (**agender**). Others may experience a partial connection to maleness or femaleness, understood within some communities as **demi-boys** and **demi-girls**. Others experience gender as shifting and changing over time, which may be labelled as **genderfluid**, or **genderflux**. Ultimately someone's experience of gender may be quite idiosyncratic, and there has been a wide range of terms constructed and explored in relation to this. These categories are shifting, overlapping, and impossible to learn in a static, systematic way. More important and practical is to communicate with an individual, and allow them to express the terms and language they use in relation to their gender.

---

7   In this version of the acronym, the 'I' stands for intersex, and the 'A' stands for asexual/aromantic (not feeling sexual or romantic attraction to people, respectively), or agender (see non-binary in this glossary). While 'A' has stood for 'allies' in some contexts, this has also been heavily criticised by many members of the LGBTQ community for ultimately including within the acronym people who are not a gender or sexuality minority.

Passing: This term can be understood in two ways. The first relates to how trans people may be read as the gender they identify with. Thus, a trans woman who is viewed as a woman by other people in society may be said to be 'passing'. Whilst many trans people may strongly desire to pass, it is also problematic if trans people who do not or cannot pass are misgendered or seen as 'less real'. Some view the term 'passing' in this context as problematic, feeling that it implies subterfuge, as in passing oneself off as something one is not. 'Blending' has been proposed as an appropriate alternative, but has yet to be broadly adopted.

The second interpretation of passing is when a trans person remains 'in the closet' concerning their gender identity. An example would be a trans woman 'passing as male'. This may be out of fear of rejection, ridicule, stigma, violence, loss of family, employment, or housing, or otherwise not feeling ready or safe to change their presentation.

Queer: This was originally a word that simply meant 'odd' or 'strange', and was later deployed as a pejorative slur, particularly against feminine or gay men. Contemporary usage of queer is no longer as simple, as it is now seen as an offensive term by some, whilst it has been 'reclaimed' by others. Many LGBTQ people now use the word queer as an identity category or term of endearment.

Within a medical context, one must be sensitive – it would be ill-advised to call someone queer or even ask them specifically if they are queer, as a strong negative association is still the case for many, particularly older individuals. However, if someone *says* that they identify as queer then this is perfectly acceptable. 'Queer' has come to be deliberately ambiguous, and ultimately communicates that the individual is simply not straight, and/or not cisgender. More specific details about the individual's relationship with gender identity or sexuality may be complicated, or the individual may resist labels and prefer a vaguer term. Queer therefore acts as another umbrella term that can be used by people with very different experiences and feelings about gender and sexual orientation. Queer is ambiguous in another way, in that it may be used to describe one's sexual orientation, gender identity (or lack thereof), or a combination of both.

Real Life Test (RLT)/Real Life Experience (RLE): this is a period of time when a trans person lives 'full-time' as their identified gender. It is common for many surgeons to require a one-year period of RLE prior to performing phalloplasty or vaginoplasty. The basis for such a requirement has been criticised because of how the question of what it means to live 'as a man' or 'as a woman' tends to rely on stereotypical presentation and behaviour. It is *not* required for a trans person to undertake the RLE in order to be referred to a Gender Identity Clinic (GIC, in a UK context), to be prescribed hormones, or otherwise be recognised as the gender they identify with. In brief, this is a controversial policy that is only relevant in the context of some gender affirming surgeries (bottom surgeries – see above). The conception of RLE predated clinical recognition of non-binary identities, therefore the lack of a clear view as to what a RLE would look like for a non-binary person renders useless the application of this criterion in this population when assessing readiness for surgery.

GICs may instead use the term **social transition**, in order to encompass a more nuanced consideration of the overlap between bio/psycho/social changes, while also shifting away from any implication that not being open about being trans is correspondingly 'not real life'. Social transition also allows the desirable outcome to be framed in terms of what the trans person wants, rather than socially prescribed gender roles that men and women may be expected to fulfil, and which makes no space for more fluid or otherwise non-binary frames of changing gender presentation or other social factors.

Stealth: Trans people who have undergone a social (and often medical) transition can find themselves correctly gendered in all social interactions, and indistinguishable from a cisgender person. The individual may hide the fact that they are trans, to protect themselves from the risk of violence, being treated differently, seen as 'not real', or stigmatised. The opposite to being 'stealth' is 'visible' or 'out'.

Whilst many trans people have no choice but to be visible if they do not pass as their gender, others may be outspoken about being trans in order to challenge stigma and discrimination, even if it puts them at greater risk. Trans people who are stealth raise ethical nuances around language. They, and many other people with trans histories, do not *identify as* trans. This is not how they see themselves, they are 'just a man', 'just a woman', or 'just non-binary'. Some may prefer to be referred to 'having a trans history' or 'being of trans experience'. The only way to know how an individual identifies and wishes to be understood is to politely ask, *if* it is clinically relevant.

As with *passing*, some see the term *stealth* as problematic, implying that one is deliberately deceiving others; 'under cover' as it were. There is nothing 'stealthy' about a man living as a man or a woman living as a woman. **Woodworked** is a less common term (synonymous with 'stealth') that is preferred by some, as it better represents the need some feel for their trans status to be invisible.

Transfeminine: Used in reference to trans people who were assigned male at birth, but who identify more with femininity than masculinity. This may include some non-binary people as well as binary transgender women. *Femininity* (behaviours and attributes that are socially associated with women) is different to *femaleness*, i.e. *being* a woman, cis or trans.

Transgender: people who do not identify with the gender they were assigned at birth. Synonymous with **trans**. People who are non-conforming in gender presentation (such as butch women, feminine men, or drag queens) are *not* transgender *unless* they also do not identify with their assignment at birth. Prior to *transgender* coming into common use other terms have been used, and the term transgender itself may also be used in different ways. This is explored in Chapter 2. Note that, whilst gender dysphoria is indisputably recognised as justifying medical treatment, being transgender in and of itself is not a pathology (Richards *et al.* 2015).

In medical settings where trans or sexual health is not being specifically addressed, a patient's trans status is unlikely to be relevant and should not be a focus of inquiry (beyond simple measures of respectful address). Probing a client's trans status may be disrespectful or offensive and thus harm the clinical relationship. Trans people report avoiding seeking medical help due to fearing or experiencing this kind of intrusion.

Transition: This marks the point at which a person changes their role and expression to one that matches their identity, to live full-time according to their affirmed gender, in all aspects of their life: within their family, in the workplace, and in leisure pursuits. This is supported by a process that may include life changes ranging from dressing and behaving in ways affirming of their gender (social transition), to taking hormones, to surgical intervention (medical transition). For some this may necessitate severing ties with friends and family who are not accepting, and/or moving to a place where their past is unknown. Transition is therefore recognised as generally including biological (for those seeking medical assistance), psychological, and social elements.

Transmasculine: Used in reference to trans people who were assigned female at birth, but who identify more with masculinity than femininity. This may include non-binary people as well as binary trans men. *Masculinity* (behaviours and attributes that are socially associated with men) is different to *maleness*, i.e. *being* a man, cis or trans.

Transphobia: despite the *-phobia* suffix being associated with irrational fears, transphobia means hatred or prejudice towards someone based on being trans. Transphobia may be expressed in many forms, from micro-aggressions like deliberate or 'accidental' misgendering and use of a person's deadname, to more serious action like denial of access, 'outing' someone as trans, or outright beatings and murder.

Transphobic behaviour is illegal in the UK under the Equality Act 2010, and may be considered a hate crime in many instances. This protects trans people from discrimination in the workplace, and in wider society. Protection under the Equality Act does not depend upon having accessed any kind of medical supervision or service. The specific wording of the legislature is that 'a person has the protected characteristic of gender reassignment if the person is proposing to undergo, is undergoing or has undergone a process (or part of a process) for the purpose of reassigning the person's sex by changing physiological or other attributes of sex' (Equality Act 2010). Despite the present government's lack of willingness to include non-binary identities (other than by 'perception' under the Equality Act) there is strong legal opinion, provided to the Women and Equalities Select Committee, which indicates that those who have undertaken a 'part of a process' to change 'other attributes of sex', and thereby move towards a gender presentation that is not congruent with the sex assigned at birth, may be, in practice, protected against discrimination, harassment and victimisation.

Transsexual: A (dated, for many) term used to refer to someone who disidentifies with the gender they were assigned at birth, and intends to, is currently, or has undergone hormonal and surgical interventions to affirm their identified gender. When this term was created in the first half of the 20th century, there was no recognition of non-binary identities (in Western contexts); therefore, transsexual people were conceived as exclusively 'male to female' (MtF) or 'female to male' (FtM) – see 'terms to avoid' for further discussion of these abbreviations. Some individuals still use the term transsexual in reference to themselves, particularly older people. However, many may find the term insulting or out of touch due to pathologising overtones that are associated with it. Some equality legislation uses 'transsexual', but it is defined broadly in such contexts to protect trans people beyond only those who meet medicalised definitions.

Terms to avoid

'Born/natal male/female': this phrase uncritically positions the genitalia viewed at birth as representing what someone *is*. This undermines the validity of a person's gender identity if this is at odds with birth assignment. It is well established that regarding sex/gender in this way is over-simplistic, and does an injustice to the significant minority of individuals whose genders are demonstrably not represented by this singular factor (Bao and Swaab 2011, Baril and Trevenen 2014, Ezie 2011, Fausto-Sterling 1993, Gomes de Jesus 2014). In particular, the term 'women-born-women' has been used to deliberately attack and exclude trans women.

'Biologically/genetically/anatomically' male/female: similar to the previous explanation, these phrases oversimplify biological concepts to the detriment of trans people. Gender identity is not 'choice' in the same way that one might choose what to eat or what to wear. Gender identity formation occurs through processes within the brain, even if the anatomical and physiological details are often unknown and will not necessarily be the same in all trans people. These ingredients in the development of minority gender experiences are biological, and may be regarded as creating *predispositions* to a particular gender identity, but outcomes are also moulded and modified by other personality characteristics and, importantly, the individual's interactions with their social and cultural environments.

When the terms 'biological male/female' are used, it creates an unjustified and unscientific hierarchy between the validity of some biological factors over others and may, in a sense, position the trans person's (biologically determined) identity as invalid and 'not real'. We live in a society that prioritises the appearance of the genitalia at birth, and while it is true that in the majority of the population this is a strong indicator of the gender identity – it is also the case that such 'congruence' is not universal.

The problem with 'genetically male/female' goes back to Kessler and McKenna's (1978) concept of the 'cultural genitals' – without a karyotype analysis (the test to identify chromosomes, that is very rarely performed), chromosomes are simply presumed from the genitals. Even if we accept that almost all trans men have XX sex chromosomes and trans women have XY chromosomes, maleness or femaleness does not depend upon this singular biological point of difference. It is dangerous to position trans women as 'genetically male' because of how this undermines their status as women. Additionally, there exist women who were assigned female at birth and who possess a Y chromosome (Hashmi *et al.* 2008), yet their status as women is not questioned. In short, genetics alone does not determine maleness or femaleness (see *intersex*, above).

Gender Identity Disorder (GID): this was the official diagnostic term used in relation to transgender adults by the Diagnostic and Statistical Manual of Mental Disorders (DSM) in their third and fourth editions, but was dropped for the fifth edition in 2013. Experts recognised how it was deeply insulting to position an individual's gender identity as inherently 'disordered' simply because a person's sense of themselves was at odds with their body or how other people saw them. By renaming the diagnosis as gender dysphoria (as the International Classification of Diseases (ICD) similarly intends to with 'gender incongruence' in their next edition), it is *distress* that requires addressing, rather than gender identity itself. In place of the out-dated perception of trans as a disorder, it is increasingly being viewed as just another aspect of human variation.

MtF/MTF, FtM/FTM: these stand for 'male-to-female', and 'female-to-male', respectively, to indicate people assigned male at birth who transition to be a woman, and vice versa. Many trans people still use these terms to describe themselves, and may easily disagree with these being 'terms to avoid'. However, these terms have also been criticised for implying that trans people 'change' from one sex into another.

'Sex change' (or 'sex swap'): this term carries connotations of an insensitive, sensationalised approach towards trans people. There have been many different terms to refer to the surgical interventions that trans people may access to address embodied gender dysphoria, including 'sex reassignment surgery', 'gender reassignment surgery', 'genital reassignment surgery', 'sex realignment surgery', 'gender confirmation surgeries' and 'gender affirmation surgeries'. 'Sex change' is particularly limited because it ignores how (medical and/or social) gender transition is a process, rather than a sudden 'change'. It also implies that being trans is for a man to 'turn into' a woman or vice versa, rather than the trans person having been their gender all along, but mislabelled and misrecognised due to their genitalia and appearance (being *misgendered*, see above).

'Shemale' / 'tranny': these words are among the most offensive and unprofessional terms, used to denigrate trans people, particularly trans women. Whilst a small number of individuals may (as with *queer*) reclaim them as an act of defiance or empowerment against stigma and discrimination, these are words that should never be used by a healthcare provider.

Transgendered: an older term that is synonymous with trans-gender, though many trans people now find this offensive. Transgender is an adjective, in that it describes an attribute of a person (like 'tall', 'thin', etc.). Adding 'ed' to the end transforms 'transgender' into a verb, which implies being trans is something 'done to' an individual. To illustrate the problem, it is typical to talk of 'gay people' but thoroughly jarring and bizarre to hear 'gayed people'.

Transgenderism/transsexualism/transgenderist: these terms have a highly clinical and pathologising history associated with them, and carry a significant implication of trans people being mentally disordered, contrary to contemporary understanding of trans identities (Richards *et al.* 2015).

'Transgenders'/'a transgender': similar to the problem with 'transgendered', these examples transform the adjective 'transgender' into a noun. This has a deeply offensive connotation for many trans people, as it erases all other aspects of their personhood. This is similar to the difference between an individual talking about 'gay people' in comparisons to 'gays' or 'a gay', which in contemporary usage may be understood as ignorant or homophobic.

Transman/Transwoman/Transpeople: this example is subtle, as the distinction is made from 'trans man' and 'trans woman' (with spaces), which are standard terminology. As already mentioned, transgender is an adjective that acts to describe the man or woman in question. Adding trans as a prefix functions to create a new word, which can be problematically used to position trans men and women as outside of the categories of men and women (i.e. 'men and transmen'). These words were historically used within the community and are still by some, but they have been criticised and should be understood as dated.

Conclusion

With regards to the 'terms to avoid' in this chapter, it is important to remember that different trans people will have different views on language. Some trans people, particularly those who are newly out, may use any of these words to describe themselves, and clinicians should avoid 'correcting' their patients on how they identify or understand themselves. Likewise, some people might take issue with some of the words that are in the first half of the glossary (friction around some terms such as queer being specifically highlighted). Ultimately the 'correct' terminology is whatever the trans person uses to describe themselves. However, in contexts outside of practitioner/service-user interactions (such as discussions with colleagues, or the writing of reports) it is important to use sensitive and up-to-date language, being aware of the explanations given in this chapter.[8]

---

8 A training resource for primary care practitioners on gender variance which earns Continuing Professional Development (CPD) credit can be found at: http://elearning.rcgp.org.uk/gendervariance

Chapter 2

Fundamental Concepts

Sex, Gender, and Transgender History

This chapter will establish a nuanced understanding of the features collectively referred to as 'sex' and/or 'gender'. Sex and gender are so fundamental to both social organisation and lived experience that it is easy to assume that a common-sense approach or basic biological knowledge are adequate. The first section of this chapter will highlight the importance of deeper consideration.

Following this, the history between the trans population and institutional medicine is outlined and contextualised. It is vital to frame why many trans people are anxious about seeking support from clinicians. Many people feel unable to be totally candid, due to fears that access to care may be threatened if clinicians do not judge them to be 'trans enough'. It is never the service provider's job to 'suspect' their trans patient of 'lying', or to expect service users to 'evidence' their trans-ness. Rather, understanding the systematic context can empower practitioners to build rapport, and earn the trust and respect of patients through their sympathy and understanding.

Transgender history can help clinicians empathise with feelings of anxiety around **gatekeeping** practices – where practitioners ultimately decide who gains access to what interventions. Under current medical guidelines, undergoing a medical transition requires a diagnosis. Because Gender Identity Clinics currently use the 10th edition of the International Statistical Classification of Diseases and Related Health Problems (ICD-10), service users in the UK are technically diagnosed with 'transsexualism', though, as the previous chapter recognised, this is problematic language (and will be updated in the ICD-11). The diagnostic description is given later in this chapter, with more information on diagnostic manuals. It is important that practitioners recognise that the notion of 'diagnosing a transgender identity' has been heavily criticised, both within medicine (Richards *et al.* 2015) and by the trans population. Currently, the act of diagnosis is needed in order to justify medically necessary interventions in the alleviation of gender dysphoria, but this is ultimately administrative as dysphoria is determined by self-declaration. Only the service user themselves can ultimately articulate if hormones and/or surgeries are right for them, as there are no 'essential' external signs of being 'really' trans or not that a practitioner can use to 'exclude' a diagnosis. In short, while the patient communicates the symptoms of gender dysphoria, there are no corresponding signs or investigations. The GIC practitioner's central role is careful documentation of self-reported chronology. The now-famous case studies at the end of this chapter illustrate how a top-down, authoritarian practice can seriously fail patients, particularly in the context of gender. By learning lessons from the past of trans healthcare, improvements can continue based on what trans patients report working for them. While the process of diagnosis currently only occurs in the context of GICs, practitioners are asked by GICs to provide hormone prescriptions, and in some cases, can also need to provide such prescriptions prior to a formal diagnosis. This is addressed in detail in Chapter 7.

Of course, access to hormones and surgeries has been quite literally life-saving for many trans people. It is important to recognise that highlighting problems found within medical practice is not to demonise healthcare professionals. Every person – regardless of intellect or training – is a product of their social environment, and so even the most well-intentioned person can internalise and uncritically reproduce behaviour and beliefs that are potentially problematic or harmful. Reflective practice can minimise this.

Sex and gender

We are taught from early childhood what 'boys look like' and what 'girls look like'. We learn one way or another that boys have penises, and girls have vaginas. This is the central factor used to label what gets called a person's *sex*, used to indicate biological differences between males and females. But which differences? 'Sex' is a collection of different factors. These include genitals (penis and vagina), gonads (testes and ovaries), internal reproductive structures (womb, fallopian tubes, epididymis, etc.), hormone ranges (testosterone and estrogen, but also others such as progesterone, which also vary across the life course), and secondary sexual characteristics (body hair growth patterns, breast tissue, fat distribution, musculature, voice pitch, and so on).

In contrast, *gender* originated as a linguistic concept, with nouns categorised in some languages as masculine, feminine, or neuter. Some professionals were affronted by the concept of *people* being described as having genders. As recently as 1991, a letter published in the *Journal of the American Medical Association* complained how the writer was 'disturbed' by the journal's use of the word gender, and that sex was the 'correct' and 'only' term to mean 'the biological characteristic of being male or female' (Fletcher 1991, p.2833). The response from the editor pointed out how the dictionary gave sex as the first meaning for gender, but did not mention gender under the definition for sex. They also stated that 'gender signifies an individual's personal, legal, and social status without reference to genetic sex; gender is a subjective cultural attitude while sex is an objective biological fact' (Iverson 1991, p.2833).

Our understanding and discussion of gendered biology, identity, and statuses has developed significantly beyond this. Some people make the attempt to demarcate language, saying that the words 'male' and 'female' refer to sex, while 'man' and 'woman' refer to gender. This can sometimes be useful with data collection. In practice, these terms are often deployed interchangeably, and these words can sometimes be used to refer to anyone who identifies as such, regardless of medical or legal status. It is reasonable to consider all men as male, and all women as female (regardless of whether they are cis or trans) because of how sex and gender are socially entangled concepts. Attempts to talk about 'female men' and 'male women' only serve to confuse, and/or offend, and have also been historically deployed to attempt to exclude trans people from being recognised as 'real' men and women.

Many have argued that 'sex is biological, gender is social'; that while sex is between your legs, gender is between your ears. This model of understanding has significant limitations and shortcomings. Firstly, the meaning we attach to physiology (sex) is also, inevitably, socially produced. Physiology does not have pre-social meaning – and indeed, the different understandings of sexed bodies over time illustrate this.

The historian Thomas Laqueur makes the case in his book *Making Sex: Body and Gender from the Greeks to Freud* (1990) that, until the early 19th century, it was common for men and women to be viewed as a single sex, instead understood in relation to 'perfection'[1]. Laqueur details how:

> Galen...demonstrated at length that women were essentially men in whom a lack of vital heat—of perfection—had resulted in the retention, inside, of structures that in the male are visible without. Indeed, doggerel verse of the early nineteenth century still sings of these hoary homologies long after they had disappeared from learned texts:
>
> though they of different sexes be,
>
> Yet on the whole they are the same as we,
>
> For those that have the strictest searchers been,
>
> Find women are but men turned outside in.

(Laqueur 1990, p.4)

It is easy to want to dismiss such accounts as empirically ignorant, and simply a product of a time with less nuanced scientific enquiry. However, it is prudent to avoid assuming that we have finalised our understandings of sex, and/or gender. It is worth considering how dogmatic certainty in the two-sex model – already recognised as over simplistic – may be viewed similarly in the future as a socially produced artefact of its time. Recognition of intersex variations (Fausto-Sterling 1993, 2000, 2008) clearly shows that sexual differentiation is not binary. One in 4500 cisgender women may be diagnosed with Müllerian agenesis[2], which results in complete or

---

1   In sexist fashion, men's bodies were considered 'more perfect' than female bodies by scholars in antiquity.
2   Also called Mayer–Rokitansky–Küster–Hauser syndrome, or MRKH.

partial absence of the uterus, cervix, and vagina – yet their status as women is not debated or challenged. The same is true for women with Complete Androgen Insensitivity Syndrome (CAIS), who are assigned female at birth based on external genitalia, yet possess XY chromosomes[3]. CN Lester considers trans bodies and biological sex in saying:

> The body of a trans woman who has pursued hormone therapy and surgery might combine XY chromosomes, higher levels of oestrogen and progesterone with concurrent lower levels of/ lower sensitivity to androgens, no testes, a prostate, a vulva and vagina, little body hair, no facial hair, breasts and curves. When looking at all the different parts of her physical make-up, what counts as 'biological sex'? All of these categories are sexed, and all are 'biological'. Why would any one category – chromosomes for example – be given precedence over another? and why should it be a problem if some bodies combine a mix of traits?

> (Lester 2017, p.66)

To give another historic example that illustrates *sex* as socially constructed, we can consider the historic relationship with sexuality. As explained in Chapter 1, we now understand sexuality and sex/gender as different – that sexual desires, sexual behaviours, and a person's sexual orientation are not dependent on our bodies, or gender identities. However, Randolph Trumbach accounts how under the paradigm in 18th century Britain, there were:

> two genders – male and female – but three sexes – man, woman and hermaphrodite. All three biological sexes were supposed to be capable of having sexual relations with both males and females. But they were presumed, of course, to have sex ordinarily with the opposite gender only, and then only in marriage, so as to uphold

---

3   A full consideration of intersex conditions and the similarities and differences with trans identities are beyond the scope of this book. Historically and politically, intersex and trans patients have been treated very differently, and faced different problems with medical care. For example, while access to surgeries has been heavily policed and difficult to access for the trans population, intersex activists have drawn attention to the still-prevalent practice of surgical intervention on intersex infants' genitals for cosmetic purposes only. Often this is done without parental consent, and judged by the intersex individual on reaching adulthood to have been invasive, non-consensual, and detrimental (with impacts such as inability to orgasm).

the Christian teaching that sexual relations were supposed to be primarily procreative.

(Trumbach 1993, p.112)

The way this worked in practice was that any 'hermaphrodite'[4] had to permanently choose to live as male or female. Men who had sex with men (for example) could find themselves classed as hermaphrodites because 'a sexual appetite for women' was positioned as essential to the male *sex*. However, men who had sex with men only caused their maleness to be questioned *if* they breached the patriarchal order, whereby older masculine men penetrated younger, more feminine men and boys. At that time, same-sex desire was yet to be associated with an identity, but was 'sinful' behaviour that anyone could fall prey to. Both men and women who had sex with others of the same sex could be positioned as hermaphrodites, however women were more likely to be medically examined by doctors for signs of physiological difference.

Over time, the third sex category 'hermaphrodite' increasingly came to be used symbolically. When used about a man, 'hermaphrodite' came to mean someone effeminate who desired men, without implying genital difference. This was a shift from the three-sex/two-gender system, to a three-gender/two-sex system[5]. The third gender was the 'Molly', an early-modern identity that can be related to gay men and trans women. This is related to how sexuality and gender identity have been confused in modern contexts – historically, same-sex sexual behaviour functioned to redefine one's sex (seen as indicative of embodied difference), and then later, one's gender (the identities people held or were labelled with). In summary, historically, sexual attraction was an 'essential' part of an individual's sex – yet this is no longer the case.

---

4   As noted in Chapter 1, this has come to be an offensive and now-antiquated term for intersex people, further illustrating how the meaning behind sex-related language shifts.

5   This is following Trumbach's understanding that demarcates sex and gender, which we have already begun to unpack. Trumbach argues that a fourth gender category also came to form, the 'Sapphist' or 'tommy' – the female counterpart to the Molly, and arguably an early-modern precursor to lesbian identities.

Sexual orientation has been disentangled from sex, illustrating that what sex *means* is dependent on society.

Recognising that sex is socially constructed is not to deny that material reality exists – simply that the meaning ascribed to biology occurs as a social process, and this has changed and continues to change over time. It is only one model (which this book problematises) to consider genitals as sex, sex as biology, and biology as 'truth'. *Because* sex and gender are not distinguished in everyday life, proclaiming a person to be a man or a woman on the basis of appearance, when inconsistent with their *identity,* can cause serious harm. For example, if we take 'sex is biology, gender is identity' to its logical conclusion, one may then describe a trans woman as having a 'female gender identity', but a 'male sex'. This is deeply problematic. Language matters hugely, because of how this allows trans women to not be seen as 'real' women, because her 'sex' (by this model) is given uncritical and unscientific primacy in deciding how she is socially understood, and indeed, medically treated. There is no medical need for genitals and other anatomical and physiological factors to be uniformly categorised as 'male', or 'female'.

This also neglects the fact that gender identity formation and negotiation is inevitably a biological process (as well as impacted by the social world) due to occurring through the brain (Winter *et al.* 2016). Yet, all trans people are deserving of respect and equal treatment regardless of the possible explanation (or explanations) that underlie identity – particularly given the significant distress which many trans people experience that only transition can relieve. Further, that 'conversion' or 'reparative therapy' is demonstrably and ubiquitously understood to be harmful. As with sexual orientation (Wilson and Rahman 2005), evidence implicating a complex biological causation is significant (if not pinpointed).

Certainly, cis and trans women may have differential health needs in many circumstances, just as any one woman may have from another woman. This is likewise true for cis and trans men. Recognising an individual's biology and healthcare needs can be done with precision without trying to separate sex from gender in a way that is socially harmful, scientifically reductive, and over-simplifying.

Attempts to separate sex and gender also have practical implications for healthcare. If we consider medical contexts where a trans woman's gendered physiology is relevant, she may well have a vagina, breasts, and estrogen and testosterone levels within a (cisgender) female range. For her 'sex' to be declared as 'male' would only cause confusion and misinformation even under a system attempting to pull sex and gender apart. This raises the question of whether it would be equally confusing if a trans person who has undergone no embodied changes from their assignment at birth had a different gender marker on their medical records. This ultimately illustrates the problem with assuming all men and women share the same biological configurations of all other men and women. In many health contexts, men and women can and should be treated the same. When gender is relevant, more information is needed than an 'M' or 'F' can communicate.

We can think of a middle-aged woman without breasts being prompted for mammograms, or women without cervixes being prompted for smear tests, both cis and trans. A patient's individual needs are always negotiated through conversation, and information on patient records. Women may need to say that they have had a mastectomy, or a hysterectomy for example, in certain contexts. Likewise, there are some medical contexts where a trans person may need to discuss their trans status, such as surgical aftercare following genital surgery.

For trans women, to be labelled as having a 'male sex' not only risks being confusing for health practitioners, but also 'outs' a trans person to anyone who sees her information, risking stigma and discrimination. There is also the issue that 'sex' can often be considered 'more real' than gender, due to sex's association with natural scientific and medical scientific research, adding a certain cultural clout. This means that the example of a trans woman being positioned as having a 'male sex' also erases the huge significance of her identity, because of how the physiology of genitalia is given primacy over neurophysiological processes within the brain, that makes trans identities possible – regardless of causation. Note that, while causation is uncertain and multi-faceted, it is certainly clear that being trans is not a 'choice'. Claiming a label to describe oneself may be socially negotiated and chosen, but this is very different – one's internal felt-sense of gender is not 'decided'. Because it is extremely well-recognised that experiencing gender dysphoria is not a matter of choice, there is no debate about the validity of transgender transitions being funded by the NHS.

Despite this, there is little purpose to research that looks to make claims of exact causation of being trans (or being gay, bisexual, etc.). The only motivation for researching the cause of a phenomenon is if one would wish to prevent it from happening, which quickly strays into the dangerous territory of eugenics. This also illustrates perhaps the largest problem with calls to accept trans (and LGB) people on the basis that it 'cannot be helped'/is not a choice. Relying on this argument suggests it is *only* because it cannot be helped that it should be accepted, implying there is something intrinsically negative about gender identity or sexuality diversity. In short, while one's felt-sense of gender is not a choice, in terms of acceptance and rights, it should not matter even if it was. Further, the spectacular complexity of gender identity makes it highly likely that no singular mechanism or explanation will be applicable to all trans people.

The connection between sex and scientific research can also mean appeals are made to objectivity – the notion that science does not make value judgements. However, scientific knowledge (whether the natural sciences or social sciences) must pass through the lens of human perception, which is constructed through our language, our cultural contexts, our backgrounds and values. We risk significant bias when we assume that science is de-facto value neutral. Reflecting upon the history of medical practice also provides poignant evidence of the dangers of this.

The history of the medicalisation of trans people

Early sexological research of the late 19th and early 20th centuries attempted to name, disentangle, and treat diversity in gender identity and sexual orientation. At that time, 'attraction to the opposite sex' was still viewed as fundamentally exclusive to each gender – any man attracted to men would bring his 'maleness' into doubt (and vice versa). Prior to the ubiquity of the term homosexuality, same-gender desire was also termed 'sexual inversion' (Ellis 1927), positioning homosexual men as having a female 'soul', or essence, within a male body. Confusingly, this meant that gay men and trans women (to use contemporary language) were put on a single spectrum of sexual inversion, with trans women simply considered 'more extreme' (Pauly 1965). Clear differentiation between homosexuality and 'transsexuality' (the earliest term used specifically about trans people) was only to come several decades later.

Variation in sexuality and gender has existed cross-culturally and throughout human history (Herdt 1993). Growing research interest across Europe during the late 19th and early 20th centuries meant the terms used to describe trans people underwent many revisions. The German physician and sexological researcher Magnus Hirschfeld was responsible for first using 'transvestite' to refer to men wearing women's clothing (Hirschfeld 1910). This did not distinguish between people who did so for entertainment, for sexual pleasure, or to fulfil expected gender roles and constitute oneself as a woman, or to alleviate dysphoria[6]. In 1923, Hirschfeld used the term 'transsexualismus', which translates to 'psychic transsexuality' (Hirschfeld 1923). This aimed to get at individuals who desired, or underwent genital surgery in addition to cross-gender presentation.

The American David Cauldwell translated Hirschfeld's term, introducing the English word 'transsexual' in his book *Psychopathia Transsexualis* (Cauldwell 1949). Almost all recognition and research at that time was of transsexual women (that is, people assigned male at birth). This was despite extensive historical examples of individuals assigned female at birth identifying themselves consistently as male for their entire lives from early adulthood (Cromwell 1999). The earliest known case of 'modern' surgical intervention was the masculinisation of the external genitalia of Herman Karl (assigned female at birth) in 1882. Karl's sex was officially recognised as male by the Prussian state (Bullough and Bullough 1993, Lester 2017).

In the first few decades of the 20th century, access to surgery for treatment of 'transsexualism' was extremely rare, and regarded as experimental. The earliest known vaginoplasty (construction of a vagina) occurred in 1931 for one Dora Richter, who was a

---

6 In simple terms, dysphoria is the often-extreme feeling of distress or discomfort that trans people may experience in relation to being positioned as the gender they were assigned at birth.

patient of Magnus Hirschfeld. Many of the earliest developments of transgender treatment were by Hirschfeld and his staff at the *Institut für Sexualwissenschaft* (Institute of Sex Research), which operated from 1919 until its targeted destruction by the Nazis in 1933. The most iconic photographs of Nazi book-burnings are of the library of Hirschfeld's institute, who was lecturing in the United States at the time. Hirschfeld never returned to Germany, settling instead in Nice, where he died on his 67th birthday, in 1935.

There was still much uncertainty around the ethics of hormonal and surgical treatment for trans people – Cauldwell advocated against physical interventions, claiming that 'transsexuality' should be regarded as a mental disorder and addressed only with therapy. However, this position did not stand the test of time. One of the earliest medical practitioners to write academically about how trans people could not be 'changed' through therapy, but only helped through hormonal and surgical interventions, was Michael Dillon, himself a trans man, who published *Self: A Study in Ethics and Endocrinology* in 1946. The further legitimisation of hormone prescriptions and surgeries to the wider medical establishment is owed to the work of Harry Benjamin, who advocated for such access based on his highly influential research (Benjamin 1954, 1966, 1967; Benjamin and Ihlenfeld 1973). In his book *The Transsexual Phenomenon*, Benjamin conceived of the Sex Orientation Scale (SOS)[7] to attempt to subdivide transsexuality based on the severity of dysphoria. Whilst no longer used due to the limited and dated conceptualisation of trans identities, this was an important step as Benjamin recognised the potential for trans people not to *universally* require surgical alteration of their bodies to be legitimised, comfortable, and healthy.

Trans people received a huge boost in visibility in the early 1950s, due to media reporting on the transition of Christine Jorgenson. As Susan Stryker put it, 'in a year when hydrogen bombs were being tested in the Pacific, war was ranging in Korea, England crowned a new queen, and Jonas Salk invented the polio vaccine, Jorgensen was the most written-about topic in the media.

---

7   Rather misleadingly named by modern standards, as this was not meant to measure sexual orientation – as the similarly constructed Kinsey Scale did, which was published earlier, in 1953.

Her story demonstrates yet again how historically contingent attention to transgender phenomena really is' (Stryker 2008, p.47). *The New York Daily News* ran a front-page story on 1 December 1952 on Jorgensen's transition, with the headline 'Ex-GI becomes blond beauty: operations transform Bronx youth'.

The media narrative around Jorgensen was very different to trans representation today, with her case initially reported as 'a rare physical condition in which her 'true' femaleness was masked by an only apparent maleness' (Stryker 2008, p.49). Jorgensen's media attention resulted in many more individuals reaching out to her directly, seeking advice on how to access hormones and surgeries so that their bodies could be aligned with their senses of self.

Very different to Christine Jorgensen, yet also a hugely important figure in transgender history, was Virginia Prince. Prince was born in the United States in 1912, and assigned male at birth. She had a career as a postdoctoral researcher in pharmacology. In her early life, she considered herself a transvestite (or cross-dresser). At the age of 30, despite the social climate in 1942, she was advised by her psychiatrist to accept herself, rather than consider herself 'sick' or 'deviant'. This influenced Prince's future work to help other trans people accept themselves (Prince 1979). Prince reshaped how particular terms were used in relation to the wide range of individuals we now collectively refer to as trans. Prince fostered a distinction between 'transsexuals' (such as Christine Jorgensen) who, by definition at the time, accessed surgery and hormones, and 'transgenderists' such as Prince herself, who did not access medical interventions but transitioned socially. Prince came to live full-time as a woman from 1968, until her death in 2009 at the age of 96.

Prince did an enormous amount of work to help create some of the earliest community organisations of cross-dressers[8], and founded the magazine *Transvestia* – which ran from the 1960s through to the 1980s. By modern standards there were many issues with Prince's assertions – such as transvestites being a term she used exclusively about heterosexual 'men', strictly

---

8   By today's standards, many of the cross-dressers of this time may have not identified as men. 'Cross-dresser' and 'transvestite' simply were the language people had available to articulate their experiences of cross-gender identification or gender diversity (for older people in particular, this can still be the case today).

excluding homosexuals. Transsexuals and 'transgenderists' were also simplistically separated, as there was still no recognition of potential uncertainty, or complexities around desiring medical intervention. Like the medical establishment, Prince was of her time and equally constrained by gender identity and sexuality being bundled together. However, the term 'transgender' was to gain traction in large part due to Prince, and she also clearly illustrated how the desire to have one's gender recognised and legitimised did not have to centre on medical interventions for everyone (even while essential for the wellbeing of some).

Diagnostic manuals

Despite early 20th century research and medical interventions, and Jorgensen's impact in the 1950s, it would only be in the mid-to-late 1960s that medical diagnostic manuals would recognise gender diversity in any way. The two most significant manuals in relation to trans care are the *International Statistical Classification of Diseases and Related Health Problems* (ICD), and *the Diagnostic and Statistical Manual of Mental Disorders* (DSM). Transsexualism was only specifically recognised in 1975 and 1980, respectively. The below tables (adapted from Drescher *et al.* 2012, pp.570–572) illustrate how terminology has developed and changed between different editions:

Table 2.1: Diagnoses applied to trans people
in different editions of the ICD

Edition	Parent category	Diagnosis name	Code
ICD-6 (1948)	N/A	N/A	N/A
ICD-7 (1955)	N/A	N/A	N/A
ICD-8 (1965)	Sexual deviations	Transvestitism	302.3
ICD-9 (1975)	Sexual deviations	Transvestism	302.3
		Transsexualism	302.5

Edition	Parent category	Diagnosis name	Code
ICD-10 (1990)	Gender identity disorders	Transsexualism	F64.0
		Dual-role transvestism	F64.1
		Gender identity disorder of childhood	F64.2
		Other gender identity disorders	F64.8
		Gender identity disorder, unspecified	F64.9
ICD-11 (tbc, ~2018)	?	Gender incongruence of adolescents and adults	?
		Gender incongruence of children (proposed)	?

Table 2.2: Diagnoses applied to trans people in different editions of the DSM

Edition	Parent Category	Diagnosis Name
DSM-I (1952)	N/A	N/A
DSM-II (1968)	Sexual deviations	Transvestitism
DSM-III (1980)	Psychosexual Disorders	Transsexualism Gender identity disorder of childhood
DSM-IV (1994)	Sexual and gender identity disorders	Gender identity disorder in adolescents or adults Gender identity disorder in children
DSM-IV-R (2000)	Sexual and gender identity disorders	Gender identity disorder in adolescents or adults Gender identity disorder in children
DSM-5 (2013)	Gender dysphoria	Gender dysphoria in adolescents or adults Gender dysphoria in children

The description given of 'transsexualism' under F64.0 is:

A desire to live and be accepted as a member of the opposite sex, usually accompanied by a sense of discomfort with, or inappropriateness of, one's anatomic sex, and a wish to have surgery and hormonal treatment to make one's body as congruent as possible with one's preferred sex.

(World Health Organization, 1992, no pagination)

This fails to recognise the existence of non-binary people, or that many binary trans people may not wish for (or be able to have) surgery/ies for a wide number of possible reasons. This does not prevent such people from being able to access appropriate care for their gender dysphoria, as practitioners can apply this diagnostic category flexibly – recognising that transgender healthcare has progressed dramatically in the 18 years since the inception of this definition.

These tables show that, over time, clinicians have come to recognise gender diversity is not pathological in and of itself. If an individual experiences significant *distress* in relation to their body, it is this distress that necessitates treatment. The changes in terminology reflect this vital development in medical understanding. Despite such medical legitimacy, it would only be with the Gender Recognition Act of 2004 that would allow trans people to change their legal gender in the UK. This was enormously significant, yet still problematic due to the lengthy and difficult process that trans people must go through to 'prove' their genders. Additionally, one must pay a significant fee, when one may argue that the original assignment of gender was mistaken. Current UK law does not offer the possibility of gender recognition for trans people under the age of 18, or people whose gender is non-binary. Further, there are also complexities around access to equal marriage as a trans person.

CASE STUDY 1: 'AGNES'

In 1967, sociologist Harold Garfinkel wrote an influential book – *Studies in Ethnomethodology* – a sociological subfield where he conceived of how people understood their sense of reality based on their lived experiences. Garfinkel collaborated with Dr. Robert J. Stoller, an influential psychiatrist, in order to study how a person achieved their 'sex status' when this is threatened or undermined in some way (Garfinkel 2006). Their case looked at the experience of one woman, pseudonymised as 'Agnes', who had been referred to see Stoller. She accessed care at the Gender Identity Clinic at the University of California, Los Angeles (UCLA) in October 1958, at the age of 19.

Agnes explained how she had been assigned male at birth, but this had been a mistake and that she had always struggled to manage being placed in the role of 'male'. When Agnes entered puberty, she developed female-associated secondary sexual characteristics (breast growth, alto voice pitch, etc.). Weekly appointments were held to assess Agnes, and she was diagnosed with an atypical case of Testicular Feminisation Syndrome (an earlier diagnosis given to patients with Androgen Insensitivity Syndrome, an intersex condition). In March 1959, Agnes' received vaginoplasty. Her weekly assessment appointments continued until August 1959.

Agnes was firm in asserting herself as a 'natural, normal female', which contributed to her doctors' assessment of her. She was described as attractive, with Garfinkel specifically noting her 38–25–38 measurements in his writing. It was also recorded how:

> There was nothing garish or exhibitionistic in her attire, nor was there any hint of poor taste or that she was ill at ease in her clothing, as is seen so frequently in transvestites and in women with disturbances in sexual identification.

(Garfinkel 2006, p.60)

It was necessary for Agnes to communicate a textbook example of idealised femininity in order to gain legitimacy, and have her birth certificate corrected to female, as she wished. Medical scrutiny was paid to her childhood play (dolls and cooking), and particularly to her sexuality. To be legitimised as female, it was absolutely necessary at that time for her to be a *heterosexual* female.

> The penis of Agnes' accounts had never been erect; she was never curious about it; it was never scrutinized by her or by others; it never entered into games with other children; it never moved 'voluntarily'; it was never a source of pleasurable feelings; it had always been an accidental appendage stuck on by a cruel trick of fate.

(Garfinkel 2006, p.66)

Even after vaginoplasty, when asked how she felt, Agnes expressed that the significance was no greater than 'having had a painful wart that had been removed', and would also compare her penis to a tumour (Garfinkel 2006, p.66). Agnes was particularly anxious at the imagined possibility that her doctors might decide that her breasts (described as 'ample' by Garfinkel) were in fact the problem, and decide to remove those rather than her penis. Surgical intervention based on patient desire and assertion of womanhood would not have been adequate in the context of the 1950s, as this was prior to the legitimisation of gender affirming surgeries for trans people in the United States[9]. Agnes' status as attractive, heterosexual, and conservative in her attitude towards gender roles and propriety all assisted her in being legitimised as a woman by her clinicians. Being 'transsexual' would have automatically disqualified her from consideration.

In October 1966, Agnes communicated with Stoller that, contrary to all her previous assertions, from the age of 12 she had stolen estrogen pills from her mother (who was prescribed them following a hysterectomy). She communicated with the local pharmacy that she was collecting the pills on her mother's behalf, and maintained long-term access. By remarkable luck, she had begun taking the hormones at the exact time necessary to prevent masculinising puberty, and at the correct dosage. This possibility had been specifically ruled out by clinicians, due to its remarkable unlikeliness. Stoller noted that 'My chagrin at learning this was matched by my amusement that she could have pulled off this coup with such skill' (Garfinkel 2006, p.91). What this case does *not* illustrate is a need for the clinician to be vigilant against 'deceptions', but to recognise that gatekeeping practices can result in unfair restrictions. These prevent access based on clinician expectations of what women and men 'should' be like, often that non-binary people do not exist, or what history someone 'should' have, to 'really be' their gender. Clinicians may feel anxious that patients are only saying what they think the clinician wishes to hear. This is ultimately a problem caused by a system which, in practice, can result in primary care practitioners refusing to provide referrals to GICs based on their sense of what a trans person should be like. As a referral to a GIC does not mean that the patient will definitively undertake a medical transition, GPs do not need to

---

9 Earlier cases occurred almost exclusively in Europe, or in Morocco in the clinic of Georges Burou, who was responsible for great innovations in vaginoplasty.

worry that they could face any professional repercussions for making a referral, even in cases such as a patient whose family does not support their (potential) transition. It is not the role of the clinician to police the veracity of a person's gender – there are no signs or investigations by which this can be done, beyond the 'symptom' – the assertion of identity by the service user, in context. However, the GIC system means that clinicians must make their own judgements as to the stability, maturity, and ability of the service user to understand the consequences of any treatments they wish to undertake. This dialogue is necessary because of the system that requires the practitioner to be responsible for any medical interventions they recommend or prescribe.

CASE STUDY 2: DAVID REIMER – 'THE JOHN/JOAN CASE'

During the 1960s, there was academic debate around the nature of gender identity – was it fixed, or flexible? Was gender identity a learned or inherent trait? One of the leading scholars interested in these questions was John Money. Born in 1921, Money was a contemporary of Robert Stoller, and responsible for co-founding the John Hopkins Gender Identity Clinic in 1965. Money produced an extremely large research output over his career, and was responsible for introducing gender as a concept used in relation to people. This was, in particular, through a formative paper where he distinguished between the factors he termed 'biological sex', and gender as a role (Money et al. 1955).

Money also popularised the term 'paraphilia', in an attempt to replace 'perversion' with a neutral term (Money 1986). However, in contemporary medicine 'paraphilia' may be regarded as not only offensive, but unnecessarily pathologising. Paraphilia classifications have been criticised as unclear, inconsistent, and lacking rigour (Moser and Kleinplatz 2006). In relation to transgender history, Money's practices provide vital ethical lessons, and indirectly, evidence to support an unspecified role for neurobiology in gender identity, regardless of socialisation.

In 1965, identical twins, named Bruce (who later took the name David) and Brian Reimer, were born in the city of Winnipeg, Canada. Both baby boys were unproblematically assigned male at birth.

Both boys were also diagnosed with phimosis[10], and referred for circumcision at seven months old. The unconventional and now-unrecommended method used for David's circumcision was electro-cautery – the burning, rather than cutting of the foreskin. An accident resulted in David's penis being destroyed beyond any potential for surgical correction[11]. Looking for support, David's parents gained a referral to John Money's practice at John Hopkins Hospital in 1967.

Money proposed – based on his belief that gender identity was *entirely* dependent on early social learning – that David be surgically reassigned as female. This decision was also informed by Money's work on intersex conditions, with (problematic) practice of the time asserting that intersex babies should only be raised as male if the phallus would functionally penetrate during penis-in-vagina sex[12] (Duckett and Baskin 1993). Additionally, the surgical difficulty of phalloplasty compared with vaginoplasty meant the latter was favoured if the existing phallic structure was deemed insufficient (Perlmutter and Reitelman 1992). David received surgeries to remove his testes and construct a vulva, and David's parents were instructed to raise him as female, ensuring he did not know the truth of his medical history. It was argued this would ensure that David (re-named Brenda) would establish a 'typical' female gender identity. It was decided that further feminising surgeries were to wait until David was older. Annual follow-up appointments with Money were scheduled for approximately ten years. Publications discussing David's (then Bruce/Brenda) experience were pseudonymised in the medical literature as the 'John/Joan case'. Money wrote and

---

10 Phimosis is the inability of the foreskin to retract over the glans of the penis. This is normal for all penises at birth and generally non-pathological, with the foreskin only becoming retractable during childhood or adolescence. However more extreme cases can result in painful urinary obstruction.

11 Following his brother's accident, Brian's circumcision was cancelled, and his phimosis then self-resolved.

12 The reader may recognise that a couple comprised of two heterosexual people should not automatically imply that one person has a penis and the other has a vagina. For instance, a straight cisgender man may be in a sexual relationship with a straight trans woman who has not had genital surgery, as her genitals do not define either her gender or his sexuality. Conversely as an example, a gay couple may potentially have penis-in-vagina sex if comprised of a cisgender man and a trans man. This will be relevant in later discussions of sexual health.

published that David's reassignment was a complete success (Money and Ehrhardt 1972).

This was not the case. Despite his body and environment being literally crafted and controlled to 'make' him female, David consistently, persistently, and insistently rejected his assignment throughout childhood. In 1994 and 1995, David, his mother, and his wife were (re)interviewed by Professor Milton Diamond, where it was articulated how David became certain he was not female between the ages of 9 and 11, and had been trying to live up to the expectations of his parents and doctors (Diamond and Sigmundson 1997). David's parents refused Money's recommendation of vaginoplasty, but David was prescribed estrogen from the age of 12:

> She [sic] would often dispose of her daily dose. She [sic] unhappily developed breasts but wouldn't wear a bra. Things came to a head at the age of 14. In discussing her [sic] breast development with her [sic] endocrinologist she [sic] confessed 'I suspected I was a boy since the second grade'.

> (Diamond and Sigmundson 1997, p.300)

David experienced suicidal depression in relation to his gender dysphoria, and threatened suicide if required to return to John Money's practice. Both David and his brother reported how the annual clinical examinations were extremely traumatic, alleging abusive and sexually inappropriate behaviour from Money, including having the boys engage in 'sexual rehearsal play' (Colapinto 2000). David's parents revealed his medical history to him when he was 14, in 1980. The same year, David asserted himself as male (taking his name), accessed mastectomy, and phalloplasty by age 16. David later worked with Diamond and was the subject of numerous documentaries, as he wished his experience to prevent similar medical practices that happened as a result of his case (Gearhart and Rock 1989)[13]. However, tragically, David committed suicide in 2004 at the age of 38, following his long struggle with depression.

---

13 At least seven cases of coercive assignment as female following circumcision accidents have been widely reported. These occurred due to the wide influence of John Money's work that temporarily established gender as being completely malleable in infants, as the dominant view. Several of these cases resulted in successful malpractice lawsuits and large financial settlements, through the failure of coercive female assignment.

The lack of empirical evidence for Money's beliefs around gender identity underscores how the medical decisions made were incredibly problematic. The possibility that the reassignment decision was influenced by the potential for an identical twin case study report to be written to bolster support for Money's theory cannot be dismissed. David's case certainly provides compelling evidence that gender identity has some unspecified biological aspect, as gender identity was asserted despite his body and environment, as with trans people. This does not justify attempts to reason that gender identity formation is a universalised experience with a singular mechanism. It is also clear that while not solely responsible for gender, social interaction and learning do influence the internalisation and performance of gender roles (Butler 1990, 1993) which can aid in understanding why trans people may come to understand themselves and come out as trans at different points in the life course.

Chapter 3

Administration and Patient Interactions

This chapter addresses administrative processes – recordkeeping and name/title changes, and interpersonal interactions as they pertain to trans patients. Needing to see a doctor can impact some trans people before even stepping into reception, due to the potential for significant anxiety, or low expectations of knowledge or sensitivity. It is essential that administration staff interact with trans service users in a manner which is respectful, inclusive, and not distressing. Key information such as the recognition of deed polls, how to change a patient's gender marker, and specific information on non-binary inclusivity will also be made clear.

Medical service providers should recognise that there is no reliable way to know whether a patient is trans, unless the patient tells them. As with reception staff, it is important to be mindful of language use, and avoid assuming a patient's gender. How a clinician engages with a trans patient may also need more depth in certain contexts. For example, healthcare needs that are centred on gendered body parts (sexual health for example) can benefit from a trans-specific approach. All staff members will benefit from reflecting on how and why particular healthcare interactions may be experienced differently by a trans service user.

Healthcare contexts where language may be particularly prominent include mental health and therapeutic provisions. While it is firmly recognised that being trans in and of itself is *not* a mental health condition or 'disorder' (Richards *et al.* 2015), there is evidence that trans people do experience higher rates of depression and anxiety. For some patients, this will be due to a dysphoric relationship with the body (or parts of it). However, for many trans people (whether experiencing bodily dysphoria[1] or not) distress results from fear of stigma and/or violence, lack of support, and the impact of microaggressions on navigating day-to-day life. Trans people who are not out, or who struggle to be consistently recognised as their gender, may be at risk of their mental health being impacted. Trans people may also experience mental health difficulties, like cisgender people, for a range of reasons unrelated to their gender identity.

Trans people experience most other mental health conditions at similar frequencies to the rest of the population, and require help accordingly. Practitioners should ensure such care does not dismiss unrelated mental health conditions as 'transgender problems', or that a patient's gender history is automatically related *because* of being trans. Conversely, refusing referral to a GIC 'until depression/anxiety is managed' is inappropriate as GIC care may be necessary to address those experiences. At the same time, sensitively-adapted interventions (such as trans-affirmative Cognitive Behavioural Therapy) can be highly useful in building trust and rapport, synergising to form best practice.

Inclusive language in service provision

The English language is heavily gendered. A person's gender is routinely assumed from their appearance, and gender-specific phrases are used presumptively. Most of the time this isn't a problem, but it can be for many trans people. This usually takes very unremarkable and innocuous forms, such as 'Good morning sir/madam', or, if talking to a colleague about a patient, 'I have a man/lady here who…'. When one habitually 'genders' people, that is, puts them into an assumed gender category, there is a risk of getting their gender wrong, or misgendering. Many trans people are not 'read' by others as their genders (see *passing* in the glossary in Chapter 1). This may be for a wide range of different reasons. Some people will not have come out, and therefore still be navigating the

---

1   'Bodily dysphoria' is used to specify that distress a trans person may experience due to aspects of the body itself. Dysphoria may also be caused by social interactions, such as other people referring to a trans person in ways that gender them incorrectly (the wrong name, title, or pronouns).

social world with people referring to them as the gender they were assigned at birth. Other people may be out as trans, but not have altered their gender, name, and/or title on their medical records. For trans people who have not accessed hormones or surgery, it may be particularly difficult to be gendered correctly, because most people have a strongly ingrained idea of 'what men and women look like'. Finally, because there is no mutually understood 'image' of what a non-binary person 'looks like', non-binary people are near-universally assumed to be men or women, even in cases where someone is androgynous in appearance.

The single most useful adjustment reception staff can therefore make is to avoid assuming a person's gender. Someone may be wearing a dress, make-up, and come across in a feminine manner, and potentially still experience distress at being called 'miss', 'madam', 'she', etc. If they are a trans man, or a non-binary person. You may expect that if someone does not identify as a woman they would not present themselves in a feminine way, however it is important to remember that, firstly, femininity is different to feeling oneself to be female (just as many cisgender women are not especially feminine without their femaleness being scrutinised); and secondly that there may be many reasons (such as keeping safe, or avoiding stigma from family or a partner) why a trans person may present in a way more associated with the gender they were assigned at birth.

Gendered language ultimately guesses gender, based on appearance. This does *not* mean it is always best to ask someone their gender outright, or what pronouns they use, in the context of reception. Not only would this be impractical and unnecessary for most patients (who are cisgender), but this could make a trans person feel exposed or at risk in the context of an open waiting room.

The most inclusive language in service provision is gender-neutral. There does not need to be any negative intent behind gendered language for it to negatively impact upon a trans person, and gender-neutral language does not pose any harm or disrespect to cisgender patients. It is important to recognise that this is not motivated by 'political correctness', but by the evidence-based recognition that misgendering can cause documented harm (Ansara and Hegarty 2014, MacNamara et al. 2017, McLemore

2015), and that inclusive healthcare practice works to minimise this (Cole 2015).

If a patient discloses their trans status to you, it will strongly indicate your sensitivity and knowledge (which is likely to be reassuring) to respond by asking 'is the name on your record how you wish to be addressed?' and 'which pronouns do you use?'. The way these questions are phrased is important. The first question is phrased to be fitting, whether talking to someone who has changed their name or not. A patient may still choose to use a name that they intend to change in the future. The second question does not assume that a patient has changed their pronouns, or make any implications or assumptions about their gender based on their pronouns alone. If someone is just starting to explore feelings of trans identification, they may wish to continue being addressed with a name and pronouns associated with their assignment at birth, for example, even if this would often contravene what most trans people would feel is appropriate for them. Additionally, by not saying 'preferred' pronouns, this acknowledges that the pronouns a person uses are not an ambivalent 'preference', but an important dimension of respectful address[2]. There may be circumstances where a trans person needs their healthcare provider to use pronouns or a title which they *prefer* not to use, but a situation necessitates. For example, if a trans person who is not yet 'out' lives with their parents, who may open their postal correspondence, this could put them at risk. Trans patients may ask for different pronoun use in a situation-dependent manner.

Examples of gendered language

Many standard terms of respect are gender-dependent. This includes 'sir', 'ma'am', 'madam', 'miss', and so on. If you are talking about a patient in the third person, you may describe them as a 'gentleman', 'lady' or, if younger, perhaps a 'lad', or 'girl'. If greeting a patient, then phrases such as 'good morning/afternoon/evening', or 'hello, how can I help?' are gender neutral, and do not make any

---

2   Note that if talking about a cisgender person, we would simply talk of their pronouns, rather than their 'preferred' pronouns. It may be appropriate to talk of 'preferred pronouns' in a case where a person uses more than one type of pronoun, perhaps depending on context, or their feelings at a particular time – as may be the case with a genderfluid person.

assumptions. In the same way, gender-neutral third person options include 'person', 'individual', or 'patient'. It is also important to remember not to assume a person's gender when speaking to them on the telephone, where we may infer gender from the voice. Staff should recognise that a 'masculine sounding' voice that declares a female title and/or name (or vice versa) has a strong chance of being a trans patient. Do not immediately assume that there is a mistake, attempted fraud, or a 'joke' being played. Verification questions (such as address, or date of birth) are adequate for the assessment of patient identity, and staff should not create additional barriers for trans patients by assuming that their voice could not possibly belong to someone with the patient's name/gender on record.

It may sometimes be necessary to indicate a patient to a colleague. Avoid using (an assumption of) gender to point someone out. Rather than saying 'the woman in the red jacket is waiting for...' one could say 'the blonde person in the red jacket is waiting for...'. If it is clear who needs to be referred to (for example, your colleague saw you interacting with them, or was part of the interaction), avoid assuming gendered pronouns. Rather than 'he will come back in 15 minutes', say 'they will come back in 15 minutes'. Some people use 'singular they' as a pronoun (notably, many non-binary people), but this is also a polite way to refer to anyone who has not clearly articulated the pronouns they use.

When can gendered language be appropriate?

The clearest circumstance when gendered language can be used appropriately is when a patient has explicitly communicated their gender to you. If someone is a man, woman, or non-binary person, then describing them in terms of their gender is obviously appropriate. This is true whether cis or trans. Someone known to be a trans woman should be referred to using female terms (she/her, woman, etc.) just as with someone *known* to be a cisgender woman, and likewise for cis/trans men.

One might deem it reasonable to use gendered language under circumstances where a trans person does not 'pass', but is clearly presenting themselves in an unambiguously gendered way to indicate their gender. For example, if a patient is wearing a skirt/dress, make-up, and is otherwise presenting in a feminine manner, yet you would infer that she was assigned male at birth, using feminised language (madam, lady, she/her, etc.) demonstrates acceptance and validation of her gender identity. It is important to recognise that this example is still uncertain territory – the person in question may be an AMAB non-binary person and not use 'she' pronouns. This presents a potential dilemma – some binary trans people may view it as offensive to be asked their pronouns if they feel their gender presentation makes it 'obvious' how they wish to be addressed, while other people's mode of address cannot be inferred from clothing. Some research (Vincent 2016) suggests that non-binary people may tend to experience more distress when misgendered as the gender they were assigned at birth, and less distressed when misgendered as the other binary gender. This perhaps supports the use of she pronouns for the hypothetical AMAB person with a feminine gender presentation, but ultimately generalisations on this topic retain a degree of risk, and finding out a person's mode of address unambiguously is preferable where possible.

Gendered language is of little consequence to the cisgender majority of patients – the difficulty lies in the inability to recognise who is trans and who is not. Gender neutralisation thus serves as the 'safest option', particularly with new or unfamiliar patients. However, older patients, particularly any person with any form of dementia, may benefit from the specificity and familiarity of gendered language (for example, addressing them by name as Mr. X or Mrs. Y). Further, if a person's gender is made contextually clear through how they talk about themselves, gendered language is unlikely to be harmful. However, be careful to avoid inferring this from appearance alone – even a patient you have seen for many years may simply have avoided bringing up their gender identity.

It is possible that a trans person will choose to tell reception staff that they are trans, and specifically request to be recognised as the gender with which they identify. Any such request is clearly to be respected whether talking to the patient themselves, or if discussing them when they are not there.

Misgendering

Even when aware of a person's gender, it is possible to make mistakes and use the wrong name, title, or pronoun to refer to someone. There are two ways that you may recognise that you have misgendered someone – being told that you have (by the person you have misgendered, or a third person), or realising yourself retrospectively. It is important to apologise, correct yourself, and move on with the conversation. It is important to correct yourself if you misgender someone when talking with someone else about them, as this not only makes your respect consistent, but also informs who you are talking to about the person's correct pronouns.

If you are corrected by the person you have misgendered, is essential to accept the correction without challenge, as no-one can be more certain of how they should be referred to than themselves. It is also important not to 'over-apologise', which draws more attention to the person's gender unnecessarily. It is also not appropriate in a professional context to articulate to the service user if you find it difficult to gender them correctly. Ultimately adjusting one's language may take careful thought, but is important for anyone for whom being misgendered is distressing or uncomfortable.

Non-binary people and inclusive language

If a person is non-binary, this means they identify as neither male nor female. This is an umbrella term, referring to a wide range of possible different gender identities. Many non-binary people experience being called 'he' *or* 'she' as misgendering – neither fits. Likewise, many non-binary people reject 'Mr' and 'Mrs/Miss/Ms' due to all of these titles being situated within the gender binary – indicating male or female.

Many non-binary people use the pronoun 'they' in the singular form (also called 'epicene they'). This works exactly as when discussing a person whose gender is unknown. Take the below imagined conversation as an example:

Person 1: Someone left **their** umbrella behind.

Person 2: Maybe **they** will come back to look for it.

Person 1: I'll hand it in to lost property for **them**.

Some people are critical of the use of singular they as a pronoun, arguing that 'it's incorrect grammar'. This is problematic because it places arbitrary grammatical rules ahead of patient respect and comfort. It is also factually incorrect – 'they' has been used to refer to singular individuals since at least the 14th century (Huddleston and Pullum 2002). A prescriptivist approach to language is unrealistic – which is particularly obvious when one recognises that the word 'you' was historically used in a plural sense, with 'thou' being the singular counterpart (Peters 2004). Singular they is frequently found in written and spoken English through the centuries, including Shakespeare ('There's not a man I meet but doth salute me / As if I were **their** well-acquainted friend' – *A Comedy of Errors*, Act IV, Scene 3).

Other non-binary pronouns also exist, but are less commonly used. Many different examples have been independently conceived, with a modern UK history of pronouns other than 'he', 'she', and 'they' going back to at least the late 1800s. The table below will illustrate some of the more frequently used examples and their conjugations (with the more common pronoun examples for comparison).

Table 3.1: Different personal pronouns and their conjugations

	Subject	Object	Possessive determiner	Possessive Pronoun	Reflexive
He	**He** said	I called **him**	**His** file	That is **his**	He likes **himself**
She	**She** said	I called **her**	**Her** file	That is **hers**	She likes **herself**
They	**They** said	I called **them**	**Their** file	That is **theirs**	They like **themselves**
E	**E** said	I called **em**	**Eir** file	That is **eirs**	E likes **emself**
Ze	**Ze** said	I called **hir**	**Hir** file	That is **hirs**	Ze likes **hirself**
Per	**Per** said	I called **per**	**Per** file	That is **pers**	Per likes **perself**

Note: it is never appropriate to refer to a trans person (in speech or in writing) as 'it'.

A non-binary title is used increasingly in the UK – 'Mx'. This is usually pronounced as 'muks'[3] or by some as 'mixter', or simply sounded out as 'em-ex'. The letter 'x' does not imply that a person using this title has a 'mixed' gender, as the x functions as a 'wildcard' character[4]. Mx is not the only gender-neutral title – others include 'Ind' (short for individual) and 'Misc' (from the Latin 'miscellus', meaning 'mixed'), however Mx is, to date, the most common gender-neutral title used in the UK. The title is accepted for use by the Department for Work and Pensions (DWP), the Driver and Vehicle Licensing Agency (DVLA), Her Majesty's Revenue and Customs, and the NHS. **There is no need for a deed poll to change title.** The titles 'Mr', 'Mrs', 'Miss', 'Ms', and 'Mx' are not controlled by law[5], and anyone can change their title to any of these upon request without proof or documentation.

Language use in gendered medicine

The term 'gendered medicine' is used here to refer to any aspect of medical practice that depends upon engaging with aspects of a patient's physiology which are gendered. The most obvious examples would be any examination, discussion, or treatment related to genitalia, or sexual characteristics. For some trans people, the way their body parts are named and discussed can make a significant difference to their experience of a medical interaction. There can be no definitive instruction that can be applied universally. Best practice is to recognise that there may be potential for distress to be heightened, if needing to discuss a patient's health in relation to (for instance) their penis, vagina, breasts, ovaries, testicles, uterus, cervix, prostate, and so on. Many

---

3   To be precise, the pronunciation of 'Mx' is /məx/, where 'ə' is the phonetic symbol for a *schwa*. This is an unstressed central vowel – such as the 'a' in 'woman', or the 'e' in 'moment'.

4   For a more detailed look at the history of the title Mx, please see the work of Nat Titman: https://practicalandrogyny.com/2014/08/28/when-was-the-mx-gender-inclusive-title-created

5   Titles such as 'Dr', 'Lord', 'Professor', 'Sir', 'Dame', etc. are controlled by law, meaning a person is breaking the law if they use such a title without being entitled to do so.

trans patients may not mind how their physiology is discussed, but asking is important to mitigate the discomfort for those patients for whom it is relevant.

Prior to any necessary discussion, questions, or examinations, the service provider should ask the patient if it would be distressing to discuss the body part(s) in question, and if there's anything the service provider can do to make the discussion easier. It should be made clear to the patient that any synonyms or euphemisms for body parts can be used in the discussion, and to follow the patient's lead with reference to body parts. For example, a trans man who has not undergone mastectomy ('top surgery') may be more comfortable talking about his 'chest', rather than 'breasts'. The service provider should explain why their questions are necessary, and be sure to avoid unnecessary inquiries.

Changing names and gender markers on medical records

When requested, a GP is required to update a patient's title, name, and gender marker on their records. There is no requirement for a person to have undergone any kind of medical treatment (hormones or surgeries), or to have a Gender Recognition Certificate to make any of these changes.

There are virtually no restrictions in the UK over what a person can take as their name. Standard conventions include:

- at least two names (a first name and a last name)

- possible to pronounce – not composed with numbers or punctuation (besides apostrophe use in surnames such as O'Toole, or hyphens in double-barrelled names such as Sally-Anne)

- not offensive (swear words, slurs)

- not composed to imply possession of an unearned title (e.g. not changing the first name to be 'Doctor').

In the context of the UK, there is no legal process necessary to start using a new name. A deed poll is only required when changing official documents such as one's passport or driving licence. It is entirely legal for an individual over the age of 16 to make their own deed poll. This has an identical legal standing as deed polls that are purchased from limited companies (these services are therefore not necessary for a trans person to have a deed poll). The recommended template given by the UK government for a deed poll is:

> I [old name] of [address] have given up my name [old name] and have adopted for all purposes the name [new name].
>
> Signed as a deed on [date] as [old name] and [new name] in the presence of [witness 1 name] of [witness 1 address], and [witness 2 name] of [witness 2 address].
>
> [your new signature], [your old signature]
>
> [witness 1 signature], [witness 2 signature]
>
> (UK Government 2017)

Patients may also provide a statutory declaration, an updated birth certificate or other documentation rather than a deed poll – admin staff/GPs should make the name change regardless.

Once a patient has changed their name, it is a legal requirement (under both data protection law, and the Equality Act 2010) for the health provider to ensure the patient's previous name is not erroneously reproduced. It should be ensured that a patient's previous name cannot appear on a display system to call patients to appointments, prescriptions, referrals to other services, supplementary spreadsheets and databases used within the service, and so on. The new name should entirely replace the old name, not input as [original name] 'prefers to be known as [new name]', unless this is specifically what the patient has requested.

No evidence is required from patients in the UK to request a change of gender marker to be processed. A procedure guide has been produced for the National Health Applications and Infrastructure Services (NHAIS)[6], with Chapter 7 of this guide specifically dealing with trans patient record changes. The NHAIS manages patient demographic details for England, Wales, and

---

6 The full document, 'PDS NHAIS Interaction Procedures Guide' can be found here: https://uktrans.info/attachments/article/60/pdsprocdoc2_2.pdf (accessed 13/01/2018).

Northern Ireland. Following a patient advising their GP that they wish to change their gender marker (and usually name), the GP can update the patient's Personal Demographics Service (PDS) record with new details. The GP writes to the Registration Office at their Clinical Commissioning Group (CCG), who then will inform the National Back Office (NBO) to request a new NHS number is allocated. The NBO will create a new profile and NHS number for the patient, and request the records held by the patient's GP. These records are then transferred to the new profile, and forwarded to the GP. Following receipt, the GP surgery can check that all aspects of the patient's new profile align with their identity. **It is not appropriate for a trans person's gender to be listed as indeterminate (unless requested by the patient), and should be recorded as their identified gender.**

In Scotland, patients advise either their GP or Practitioner Services (a business unit of NHS Scotland). There is a population register called the Community Health Index (CHI), with all patients in NHS Scotland allocated a CHI number. The CHI number is gendered, and therefore requires a manual intervention by a staff member at Practioner Services. Name changes can be made by GPs as this can be automatically processed by CHI. Many NHS Scotland computer systems do not hold a title field, with this being automatically generated based on gender and marital status. As this is particularly problematic for someone using Mx, staff should look into the possibility of system updates where possible, with apologies and explanations given to patients whose titles cannot be processed by the system.

When a patient requests a change of gender marker, the GP should check if appropriate gender-specific screening notifications (for example, cervical screening for a trans man) can be sent to the patient automatically without being dependent upon their gender marker. Practice IT systems vary so, if this is not possible, it is beneficial to liase with IT support to make adjustments, or think creatively about how this can be best managed. For example, with the patient's consent, a practitioner could set up a note on the patient's medical records to instruct the practitioner when to notify the patient of a screening recommendation. Many practices have a history of placing all responsibility for remembering screening onto trans patients (some even requiring a waiver be signed before allowing the change of gender marker). This is arguably discriminatory, because it differentiates who receives support in the form of reminders and who does not on the basis of trans status.

Additional name change options in Scotland and Northern Ireland

Any trans person whose birth (or adoption) was registered in Scotland or Northern Ireland has the ability to have their name change recorded on their birth (or adoption) certificate. These services are optional, and not required for a name change to be accepted by the patient's healthcare providers. Changing one's name by deed poll in Scotland and Northern Ireland works in the same way as in England and Wales. A charge must be paid to the relevant authority for the specific service of birth certificate change[7]. In both contexts, a change of forename may only be performed once, and a change of surname a maximum of three times. Rules differ slightly if under 16 in Scotland, or under 18 in Northern Ireland.

Helping a patient change their passport

The process of changing the sex marker on UK passports requires a letter from a doctor. The doctor can provide this to trans patients without that patient having yet made changes to their gender marker within the NHS system, or on any other particular piece of documentation. The patient does not need to have been referred to a GIC, or have accessed, be accessing, or intending to access hormones and/or surgeries. Such a letter should indicate that the

---

7   For more information on the Scottish context of birth certificate amendment, please see: https://www.nrscotland.gov.uk/registration/recording-change-of-forename-and-surname-in-scotland

For more information on the Northern Irish context of birth certificate amendment, please see: https://www.nidirect.gov.uk/articles/recording-change-name

change of gender is intended to be permanent. A template for such a letter[8] is:

> To whom it may concern,
>
> This is to confirm that my patient, previously known as [old full name], is currently undergoing gender reassignment and as part of this process has changed [his/her/their] name by statutory declaration to [new full name]. [new name] now lives as [gender] and this change is intended to be permanent.
>
> Your assistance in making the relevant changes to your records and in preserving full confidentiality will be appreciated.
>
> Yours faithfully
>
> [Dr Name]
>
> (UK Trans Info 2017)

The possibly of an 'X' marker on passports for non-binary people is under review by the UK government, but is not possible at the time of writing. Communicate with the patient to ensure what they wish the letter to say, and double-check whether a non-binary sex marker is possible if this is desired.

Trans-affirmative therapeutic interactions

It has been empirically recognised that some clinicians continue to hold pathologising and/or negative (and often stereotyping) views of trans people, with particularly dismissive attitudes if a patient identifies outside of the gender binary (Austin and Craig 2015, Bess and Stabb 2009, Logie *et al.* 2007). This chapter has already established that sensitive language use can be a significant factor in the healthcare experiences of trans patients, and thus treatment or intervention that is heavily 'talk-focused' merits particular attention.

Cognitive Behavioural Therapy (CBT) is one of the most widely-used psychotheraputic interventions for addressing a wide range of mental health problems, such as depression, anxiety, eating

---

8   If a trans person has a Gender Recognition Certificate, this can act in lieu of a doctor's letter.

disorders, substance abuse, obsessive compulsive disoder, and other conditions. The central premise of CBT is to learn to change thinking patterns, in order to alter behaviours and their impact. In articulating a model of trans-affirmative practice, Austin and Craig (2015) highlight how explicitly indicating a validating and informed practice to a trans service user will increase the likelihood of a positive clinical relationship. They give as a potential example:

> Welcome, I'd like to take a moment to share my approach to practice with you. In keeping with clinical practice that is affirming and inclusive, I embrace a trans-affirmative approach in which all experiences of gender are acknowledged and validated. I aim to create a space for clients to safely explore, understand, and inhabit their unique experiences of gender.
>
> (Austin and Craig 2015, p.22)

It is advised that therapeutic practitioners do not 'memorise a script', as this risks coming across as insincere and overly-rehearsed. Rather, an individualised confirmation of a trans-affirmative approach in a conversational manner, open to questions and feedback is likely to be most effective. When making their introduction, the practitioner may also wish to disclose their pronouns, to highlight that they are aware of the practice of not making this assumption about others. It is also important that the individualised approach is aware of non-Western gender diversity, and appreciates the value of culturally-specific care (Maguen et al. 2005).

It is vital that mental health practitioners do not refuse trans clients on the assumption that they are not qualified or equipped to address issues that could be (or could be related to) dysphoria. There is no reason why a mental health provider cannot work with a trans person to assist with mental health prior to (if sought), during, or after a medical transition process. Mental health practitioners should be familiar with the Memorandum of Understanding (MoU) on Conversion Therapy in the UK (NHS England et al. 2015) which states that psychotherapeutic attempts to change a client's sexuality has no evidence of working, whilst being evidenced to potentially cause great harm. This Memorandum was updated in January 2017 to include gender identity (British Psychoanalytic Council 2017).

While therapists should not assume or conclude that being trans directly causes depression or anxiety, familiarity with the Minority Stress Model (Hendricks and Testa 2012, Kelleher 2009, Meyer 2003) will allow for a more nuanced understanding. This model has been used to explain how gender and sexuality minority group members often experience chronic stress because of microaggressions, prejudicial encounters, or fear of them. This can negatively contribute significantly to an individual's wellbeing.

Austin and Craig explain that trans-affirmative therapy should help service users 'recognize and understand the relationship between transphobic experiences and feelings of stress, anxiety, depression, hopelessness, and suicidality' (Austin and Craig 2015, p.24). A particularly important dimension of a trans-affirmative therapeutic practice is for the service user to have, or work to improve/gain, an affirming support network. Familiarity with different trans groups (locally, nationally, and digitally) will allow the practitioner to make recommendations for avenues a service user may wish to pursue if experiencing isolation from trans communities. You may even decide to put up a poster for a local trans or LGBTQ support group in your waiting room.

Chapter 4

The Referral Process

For those trans people who require hormones and/or surgeries, getting a referral to a Gender Identity Clinic (GIC), almost always from a General Practitioner, can be considered one of the most important and nerve-wracking steps. This is largely due to the widely different responses that trans people have reported experiencing when requesting a referral. Many GPs feel under-equipped to make a referral to a GIC, due to a lack of specific knowledge of what is needed from them – medically, ethically, or even legally. Many practitioners do whatever they can, through an informal (often internet-based) self-education. This may not only be a daunting, unstructured, and time-consuming task, but also has the undesirable knock-on effect of delaying the referral.

The impact of this is potentially grave, because of the serious difficulty that some trans patients have managing their dysphoria during waiting times. This is compounded by the fact that GIC waiting times are the longest of any specialist care due to enormous oversubscription. While NHS England has confirmed that the 18 week referral-to-treatment time standard does apply to GICs, in the worst instances, some patients have reported a wait of over five years for a first appointment. Due to the exceptionally high rate of suicide and attempted suicide among the trans population (most poignantly, dysphoric individuals with a lack of access to gender-affirming medical interventions), there is a strong ethical imperative for referral to be as quick and simple as possible, with the added benefit of minimising the draw on GPs' (or other healthcare providers') time.

This chapter will focus on referral practices to adult services. Referral for children and adolescents is specifically addressed in

Chapter 6. In most cases, patients who are 17 at the time of referral can be referred to adult services[1]. GPs should be aware that not only are the differences based on service commissioner (NHS England, NHS Scotland, or Health and Social Care Services in Northern Ireland), but also between individual GICs. This chapter will provide general guidelines to inform both service providers and service users about referral processes, and specific information for each of the Gender Identity Clinics in the UK. Some of the information given is duplicated across multiple clinics (where accurate, such as the contents of referral forms) in order to provide as complete an account as possible for those readers selectively reading about a particular clinic.

Due to the changing nature of national policy, information in this chapter risks becoming out of date (particularly reported waiting times). As a minimum, the information provides a snapshot of policy and protocols as they were during late 2017.

General information for professionals making a referral to a GIC

Due to the great heterogeneity of the trans population, it is very important not to assume that only people who look a certain way, or articulate a certain narrative of being trans, will ask for referral. Some people may be very young (although referring children and adolescents is addressed in Chapter 6) and others may be post-retirement age – there is no upper age-limit for referral to a GIC. Some people may already present as the gender they identify with, while many others will not. A person does not need to have undertaken any dimension of social transition to be referred – they may still use a name and pronouns associated with their assignment at birth, for example.

While some people may be comfortable talking to a professional about being trans and asking for referral, many are likely to be very

---

1 This may change in the future. The most recent adult consultation made the suggestion of having adult and young person services overlapping significantly, with young people being able to access adult services from the age of 16, and GIDS being able to keep patients until age 20. This is not currently possible, and finalisation of any policy change is yet to occur.

nervous – fearing a sceptical (or worse, derisory) clinician unwilling to address the request. **There are no medical circumstances which are contraindications for referral to a GIC.** There is also no need for a compulsory psychiatric assessment in order to be referred. Many people seeking referral will have struggled with their identity and experiences of gender dysphoria for many years prior to seeking referral. It is both unhelpful and ultimately not the role of the referring practitioner to establish the 'certainty' of the person seeking referral regarding their gender. Further, waiting times for first appointments with GICs are exceptionally long (which is well-recognised within the trans community) and so delays to referral may heighten experiences of distress. There is an ethical imperative for referral to be completed for all patients who request it as quickly as possible. Some people seeking referral to an NHS GIC may have accessed gender affirming medical interventions (such as hormones) via private practice. This does not disqualify them from being referred. A sizable number of patients (who can afford to) access private treatment to manage dysphoria while on an NHS waiting list, and will transfer their care to their GIC and GP to reduce personal cost once NHS appointments become available.

Further, some patients may have accessed hormones themselves via the internet and be self-medicating. This also does not exclude them from referral. In line with harm reduction practices, the practitioner should check their bloodwork, and consider the risks of harm to the patient by *not* prescribing hormones under these circumstances. The Good Practice Guidelines for the Assessment and Treatment of Adults with Gender Dysphoria (Royal College of Psychiatrists 2014) makes reference to the World Professional Association for Transgender Health (WPATH) Standards of Care (Coleman *et al*. 2012) which states that a bridging prescription[2] while awaiting assessment at the GIC may be appropriate. More information on this may be found in Chapter 7.

---

2   In this context, the bridging prescription would be either estrogen or testosterone. In a GIC context, the term 'bridging prescription' can be used to reference other prescriptions (such as finasteride, an antiandrogen) used prior to a hormone regimen. The most common meaning of 'bridging prescription' in the trans community is access to a hormonal prescription in the interests of harm-reduction, while waiting for GIC assessment.

England

There are currently seven adult GICs across England. Anyone aged 17 or older living in England can be referred to any of these clinics. The service user can choose where they want to be referred – it does not have to be the closest clinic to where they live. Service users may find it beneficial to compare the information given on different clinical requirements and practices, to inform their decision on a choice of clinic. Clinics are listed alphabetically by location.

Daventry: Northamptonshire Gender Service

Danetre Hospital, H Block, London Road, Daventry, Northamptonshire, NN11 4DY

Telephone: 01327 708147

Email: genderclinic@nhft.nhs.uk

Website: www.nhft.nhs.uk/gender-identity-clinic

Provided by: Northamptonshire Healthcare NHS Foundation Trust

Average waiting time for first appointment (October 2017): 30 months

Accessibility: Information on the accessibility of Danetre Hospital (where service-users attend GIC appointments) can be found here: www.disabledgo.com/access-guide/ northamptonshire-healthcare-nhs-foundation-trust/ danetre-hospital

This clinic provides a referral form for practitioners to complete, which can be downloaded from a link on this page: www.nhft.nhs. uk/gender-identity-clinic#venue-how-to-get-referred-tab

The Daventry clinic specifies that patients under 17 may be referred to this adult service, providing they will have passed their 17th birthday by the date of their first appointment. The service seeks advance agreement from the patient's GP to agree to undertake blood tests and prescribe hormones as advised by the GIC, and to send the results of tests to them. GPs should agree to this, in line with shared care arrangements under current protocol (more information on hormone prescription can be found in Chapter 7). This is also because the GIC is not commissioned or funded to prescribe or administer hormones directly.

The person being referred must also sign the referral form, to give their consent for the Northamptonshire Gender Service to request and access their healthcare information, if the GIC deems it relevant to the referral. If the patient does not want to sign, the referral can still be completed. In cases where a patient is unwilling to sign, the referring clinician must provide the reason for the refusal, in order for the referral to continue to be considered by the GIC.

The referral form requests a 'detailed reason for referral', and 'gender history'. The form indicates this includes age of awareness, preferences (pronouns and name), who (if anyone) trans status has been disclosed to, and whether the person is or has self-medicated with hormones. Completing this form should therefore be done collaboratively with the person asking for referral. Additionally, there is a section titled 'mental state examination'. If the professional making the referral is not a mental health specialist, they should *not* feel unable to complete this section – only basic information is necessary, and any patient requesting referral should be deemed capable of reporting on their mental health presuming no contraindications (of which gender dysphoria/a trans identity are not). No assessment/referral to mental health services is necessary for referral to be completed.

Exeter: West of England Specialist Gender Identity Clinic

The Laurels, 11–15 Dix's Field, Exeter, EX1 1QA

Telephone: 01392 677077

Email: dpn-tr.TheLaurels@nhs.net

Website: www.devonpartnership.nhs.uk/Specialist-Gender-Identity-Clinic.wesgic.0.html

Provided by: Devon Partnership NHS Trust

Average waiting time for first appointment (October 2017): 18 months

Accessibility: There is a ramp for outside access to the main building, and elevator access to The Laurels. Gender neutral bathroom space is available.

The Exeter GIC is known as The Laurels. This clinic does not provide a specific referral form, but recommends that GPs make the GIC aware of any co-existing conditions, and any risk/vulnerability factors when making their referral (such conditions do not preclude referral, or treatment by the GIC). Physical examination by the GP or blood work are not necessary for a referral to be made. In addition to GPs, The Laurels will accept referrals from other healthcare professionals, but stresses that the person being referred must be registered with a GP willing to collaborate with the individual's care. Referrals can be sent by post to 'NHS Referrals: West of England Specialist Gender Identity Clinic' at the above address. Referrals can be made to The Laurels for anyone aged 17 or older.

Prior to referral or during the wait for a first appointment, patients can contact The Laurels and be put in touch with a trans volunteer who has used the service.

Leeds: Gender Identity Service

The Newsam Centre, Seacroft Hospital, York Road, Leeds, LS14 6WB

Telephone: 0113 85 56346

Email: gid.lypft@nhs.net

Website: www.leedsandyorkpft.nhs.uk/our-services/services-list/gender-identity-service/

Provided by: Leeds and York Partnership NHS Foundation Trust

Average waiting time for first appointment (October 2017): 16 months[3]

---

3   Comprehensive data on Leeds GIC waiting times from 2014–2017 can be found here: www.leedsandyorkpft.nhs.uk/our-services/wp-content/uploads/sites/2/2017/10/gender-identity-waiting-times-q2–2017–18.pdf

Accessibility: Due to the nature of the building, Seacroft Hospital is accessible for wheelchair users.

The Leeds GIC request that an individual seeking referral be specifically referred by their GP to indicate that the GP is implicitly willing to engage in shared care practices. Leeds have a specific referral form which can be accessed here: www.leedsandyorkpft. nhs.uk/our-services/wp-content/uploads/sites/2/2016/10/gender-identity-service-referral-form.pdf

The referral form should be completed in collaboration with the individual requesting referral. The form asks for a brief summary of the reason for referral, and any past physical and mental medical history. An 'up to date mental state examination' is asked for – this does not require specialist consultation or referral to mental health services. Without contraindication (of which trans identification is not) the patient should be considered capable of self-reporting on their mental state. Additionally, any difficulties (anxiety, depression, etc.) do not disqualify an individual from referral. The referral form also asks for a brief family history, any repeat prescriptions, any acute medications within the last 12 months, and any allergies and/or sensitivities.

Controversially, the Leeds referral form asks for an up to date physical examination (including biometric values), and requests an examination of the patient's sexual characteristics[4]. No other GIC deems this examination necessary. In addition, **the patient has the right to refuse this examination, which they should be aware of**. The referral can still be made without any examination of sexual characteristics being made. Finally, the form asks for any other agencies involved (any private gender-related care accessed), and any other information the patient may deem relevant. The referral can be returned by post to 'Leeds Gender Identity Service, Management Suite, 1st Floor', followed by the address given above.

The Leeds clinic offers a voice group facilitator, who specifically provides two eight-week courses per year for people assigned male

---

4 Trans service users and activists have deemed this policy voyeuristic and medically unnecessary at the referral stage. For any patient not pursuing genital surgery, the morphology of sexual anatomy is irrelevant. For any patient who is interested in pursuing genital surgery, examination would be undertaken at a much later stage by a surgical practitioner, rather than the GP.

at birth to assist in feminisation of the voice. Day-long workshops are offered for people assigned female at birth, to assist in vocal masculinisation.

London: Gender Identity Clinic for Adults

179–183 Fulham Palace Road, Hammersmith, W6 8QZ

Telephone: 0208 938 7590

Email: PALSGIC@tavi-port.nhs.uk

Website: gic.nhs.uk

Provided by: Tavistock and Portman NHS Foundation Trust

Average waiting time for first appointment (October 2017): 14 months

Accessibility: The front entrance to the practice is on the same level as the ground floor, and is wheelchair accessible. An elevator on the ground floor is available to access the reception, on the first floor of the building. The practice has a portable ramp if needed. Gender-neutral bathroom facilities are available, one of which has double doors and is fitted to be accessible. Interpreters and British Sign Language (BSL) signers are available.

Also known as Charing Cross, this is the largest (and most subscribed) Gender Identity Clinic in the UK. Charing Cross is also the oldest UK Gender Identity Clinic, founded in 1966. This clinic provides a referral form for practitioners to complete, which can be downloaded from a link on this page: gic.nhs.uk/referrals

As with other GIC referral forms, Charing Cross asks for the reason for the referral. The form also asks whether the patient has undergone a social transition, undertaken a name change, and whether they have re-registered with a new name at the GP's surgery. A medical history is requested, together with any current prescribed or non-prescribed medications (including hormonal self-medication if relevant, contraception, or herbal medicines). An up-to-date mental state examination is asked for. If referral is being made by a GP or another specialist not involved with mental health, they should still feel able to complete this section without further consultation or referral being necessary. Without contraindication (of which trans identification is not) the patient should be considered capable of self-reporting on their mental state. Additionally, any difficulties (anxiety, depression, etc.) do not disqualify an individual from referral. The patient's mental health background is also requested, together with any forensic history[5] if known. The form asks for any other agencies involved (any private gender-related care accessed), and any other information the patient may deem relevant.

Charing Cross also asks for information from a physical health assessment as part of their referral form. This includes height, weight, waist measurement, BMI, blood pressure, heart rate, whether the patient has polycystic ovarian syndrome (PCOS) or an intersex condition, and whether they smoke, drink alcohol, or use recreational drugs (and how much). If the patient does not explicitly know that they have a diagnosis of PCOS or an intersex condition, the GP should record this as 'no'[6]. Referring physicians should note that **the referral can and should still be sent if patients do not wish to give any particular information (which they should be informed they have the right to do), or if particular information is not known.**[7] Charing Cross also requests that blood tests should be completed no more than six months prior to their first appointment. The patient should be given a computerised printout containing the following information to bring to their first assessment with them:

- full blood count

- urea and electrolytes

---

5   Where mental illness may intersect with any history of criminal offending.
6   The battery of tests that would be necessary to definitively eliminate the wide range of possible intersex variations (for example) are medically unnecessary.
7   There is no medical reason for the collection of the data under the 'physical health assessment' section of the Charing Cross referral form as part of the referral process. This is supported by the fact that no other GICs request this information at the point of referral, if at all. Additionally, information about weight and body composition would only be relevant if surgical interventions may be needed, which would need reviewing due to the length of time this would be post-referral.

- liver function tests/gamma GT

- serum calcium

- B12 and folate

- cholesterol

- triglycerides

- fasting blood glucose

- sex hormone-binding globulin (SHBG)

- FSH

- LH

- vitamin D

- prolactin

- estradiol

- testosterone

- dihydrotestosterone.

The referral can be returned by post to the Referral and Funding Team (at the address above) or by email to gic.administration@nhs. net. Charing Cross accepts referrals of patients who are 17 years and 6 months or older. Up to six months following from referral, patients receive a welcome pack from the service, and an opt-in letter. The opt-in letter requires a reply, otherwise they will be discharged. It is beneficial for GPs to inform their referee of this to ensure awareness. Service users should receive an appointment letter one month in advance of their appointment.

Newcastle: Northern Region Gender Dysphoria Service

Benfield House, Walkergate Park Hospital, Benfield Road, Newcastle, NE6 4PF

Telephone: 0191 287 6130

Email: NRGDS@ntw.nhs.uk

Website: www.ntw.nhs.uk/services/northern-region-gender-dysphoria-service-specialist-service-walkergate-park/

Provided by: Northumberland, Tyne and Wear NHS Foundation Trust

Average waiting time for first appointment (June 2017): 13 months

Accessibility: A patient information leaflet can be downloaded from the service website as a large print version.

Patients who are 17 years or older and living in England can be referred to the Northern Region Gender Dysphoria Service. Referrals are accepted from GPs and from other healthcare professionals. The service specifies that referrals should include background on the individual's physical and mental health, and any current or ongoing medications. The service does not currently have a bespoke referral form.

Nottingham: The Nottingham Centre for Transgender Health

3 Oxford Street, Nottingham, Nottinghamshire, NG1 5BH

Telephone: 0115 876 0160

Email: Nottinghamgender@nottshc.nhs.uk or not-tr.gender-services@nhs.net

Website:www.nottinghamshirehealthcare.nhs.uk/nottingham-centre-for-transgender-health

Provided by: Nottinghamshire Healthcare NHS Foundation Trust

Average waiting time for first appointment (October 2017): 18 months

Accessibility: Patients registered as disabled may be able to have travel cost reimbursed by the clinic. Contact should be made with the clinic for more information.

The Nottingham clinic will accept referrals of 16 year olds who will be 17 at the time of their first appointment. Referrals can be made by a person's GP, or from local psychological or psychiatric services – however the individual's GP must support the referral (the clinic advises that if a person's GP will not support the referral then a second opinion should be sought). The clinic also specifies that any significant mental illness (schizophrenia, bipolar disorder, etc.) should be well managed prior to attendance but that such diagnoses do not mean that someone cannot be referred and seen. It is appreciated that anxiety and depression can be strongly resultant from gender dysphoria and social stigma, so GPs and other referees should not presume that such distress can necessarily be 'well managed' prior to GIC referral.

Sheffield: Gender Identity Service

Porterbrook Clinic, Michael Carlisle Centre, 75 Osborne Road, Sheffield S11 9BF

Telephone: 0114 271 6671

Email: porterbrook@shsc.nhs.uk

Website: https://shsc.nhs.uk/service/gender-identity-service/

Provided by: Sheffield Health and Social Care NHS Foundation Trust

Average waiting time for first appointment (October 2017): 12 months

Accessibility: No explicit information is available.

The Sheffield GIC provides information about referring to their service on their website: shsc.nhs.uk/service/gender-identity-service – the clinic requests that referral information includes (in writing):

- A medical history of any past or present mental or physical health issues, and any risk assessment necessary in relation to mental health

- Any current medications

- Recent baseline blood test results:
  - full blood count
  - urea and electrolytes
  - liver function tests
  - fasting blood glucose
  - lipid profile
  - serum free T4
  - TSH
  - testosterone
  - estradiol
  - prolactin.

Sheffield accepts referrals from any commissioned NHS healthcare professional. The Sheffield service description states that those referred are 'usually' 18 years or older, implying that 17 year olds may be referred to Sheffield, as with other English GICs for adults.

Information for Welsh referrals

Wales currently does not have an NHS managed Gender Identity Clinic[8]. The Welsh Health Specialised Services Committee (WHSSC) has constructed a policy for Welsh service users to access gender identity services. At present, a slower process with additional gatekeeping is in place, in comparison to the rest of the UK. Welsh GPs are not currently permitted to make referrals directly. Following a request for a referral from a service user in Wales, the GP needs to make a referral to the patient's local Community Mental Health Team (CMHT). The local CMHT is then responsible for the allocation of funding and making the referral directly to Charing Cross GIC, in London. Welsh patients do not currently have freedom of choice about where they are treated, unlike patients in England.

---

8   Creation of a Welsh GIC has been proposed and is a likely future development
    – be sure to check the most recent available sources.

Scotland

There are currently two main GICs covering Scotland, located in Edinburgh (the Lothian Sexual Health Clinic, also known as 'Chalmers') and Glasgow (Sandyford Clinic). There are also two additional clinics – the Highland Sexual Health Clinic (also called 'Raigmore') is based in Inverness, and acts as a satellite clinic for Sandyford. The Grampian Sexual Health Clinic is based in Aberdeen, and has had a period of difficulty following the retirement of clinical staff. Therefore, as of mid-2017, the clinician and nurse who practice at the Edinburgh clinic travel to see patients at the Aberdeen clinic, once per month.

Where a Scottish service user can be referred depends on where they live in Scotland. Patients who reside in the NHS Lothian, Borders, Fife, and (at least temporarily) Grampian areas are referred by a GP to the Lothian Sexual Health Clinic in Edinburgh, provided they are 17 or older. Anyone living anywhere else in Scotland should be referred to the Sandyford Clinic in Glasgow (except for people living in NHS Highland – see under the 'Inverness' subtitle below). All Scottish referrals for people under 17 should be to Sandyford in Glasgow, regardless of location (see Chapter 6).

Service users who live under NHS Tayside self-refer to Sandyford GIC, but are also requested to ask for referral from their GP to their local psychology team for support while waiting for a first GIC appointment. The local Tayside psychologist can refer people for speech therapy and hair removal, but not for hormones or surgery. The additional step in the Tayside region is so that for service users desiring medical transition, the local psychology team can authorise local funding to pay for the Sandyford GIC appointments. Assessment by the local psychologist is also used to reduce the number of appointments necessary at Sandyford before a service user can be approved for hormone access.

Glasgow: Sandyford Clinic

6 Sandyford Place, Sauchiehall Street, Glasgow, G3 7NB

Telephone: for self-referrals – 0141 211 8137, for general enquiries – 0141 211 8130, for professional referral on a patient's behalf – 0141 211 8646

Email: sandyford@ggc.scot.nhs.uk

Website: www.sandyford.org/sandyford-sexual-health-services
/what-are-our-services/gender-identity-service/

Provided by: NHS Greater Glasgow and Clyde

Average waiting time for first appointment (June 2017):
12 months

Accessibility: NHS Greater Glasgow and Clyde has made web
resources about the service more accessible, see: www.
sandyford.org/accessibility

Sandyford GIC allows for self-referrals to be made – it is not
necessary for a GP or other health practitioner to make the referral
for a patient. An initial appointment can be arranged by telephone.

If requested, Sandyford can arrange to have the services of
Minority and British Sign Language (BSL) interpreters. The
service's information booklet (available from the service's website)
also states that Sandyford is physically accessible for disabled
people. Sandyford also possesses a health and information library,
with PCs with free internet access and print resources on gender
identity. Books can be borrowed by service users who have a local
library card in Glasgow.

Edinburgh: Lothian Sexual Health Clinic

2A Chalmers Street, Edinburgh, EH3 9ES

Telephone: 0131 536 1570

Email: not available

Website: lothiansexualhealth.scot.nhs.uk/services/gic/

Provided by: NHS Lothian

Average waiting time for first appointment (October 2017): not
available

Accessibility: No explicit information is available.

The Chalmers GIC (as the Lothian Sexual Health Clinic is also called) can receive referrals from GPs for service users who are 17 or older. **Referrals are only accepted from patients who live in the NHS Lothian, Borders, or Fife areas.** The clinic does not use a referral form, nor is information required in a referral included on the service website. GPs are advised therefore to follow the basic requirements generally asked from other GICs – an evaluation of any physical or mental health conditions/history, and any current medications.

Inverness: Highland Sexual Health Clinic

Raigmore Hospital, Inverness, IV2 3UJ

Telephone: 01463 704202

Email: not available

Website: www.nhshighland.scot.nhs.uk/Services/Pages/Sexual Health.aspx

Provided by: NHS Highland

Average waiting time for first appointment (June 2017): not available

Accessibility: No explicit information is available.

NHS Highland require patients in their area to self-refer to the Inverness satellite clinic. Here, patients can be referred for hair removal and speech therapy, and low doses of hormones may be prescribed (as a bridging prescription) while waiting for a referral to the Sandyford Clinic in Glasgow. The clinician at the Inverness clinic cannot currently approve surgical interventions, but does see patients between Sandyford appointments to provide additional support.

Aberdeen: Grampian Sexual Health Clinic

Aberdeen Community Health and Care Village, 50 Frederick Street, Aberdeen, AB24 5HY

Telephone: 0345 337 9900

Email: not available

Website: www.nhsgrampian.org/nhsgrampian/sexual_health_template.jsp

Provided by: NHS Grampian

Average waiting time for first appointment (June 2017): not available

Accessibility: No explicit information is available.

As detailed above, this clinic currently lacks clinical staff to accept referrals or provide consultations. Edinburgh clinicians currently see patients in Aberdeen one day per month, therefore service users under NHS Grampian should be referred to the Edinburgh GIC.

Northern Ireland

Northern Ireland has one adult GIC, and an adolescent service for patients under 18 years old (see Chapter 6).

Belfast: Brackenburn Clinic (Regional Gender Identity and Psychosexual Services)

Brackenburn Clinic, Shimna House, Knockbracken Healthcare Park, Saintfield Road, Belfast, BT8 8BH

Telephone: 028 9063 8854

Email: BrackenburnClinic@belfasttrust.hscni.net

Website: www.belfasttrust.hscni.net/services/GenderIdentity.htm

Provided by: Belfast Health and Social Care Trust

Average waiting time for first appointment (June 2017): three months[9]

Accessibility: No explicit information is available.

---

9   Waiting times in Northern Ireland in 2016 ranged between two weeks and 14 months. See here for detailed information: www.belfasttrust.hscni.net/pdf/How_are_we_doing_Report__2016_Final_version.pdf

On the second Tuesday of every month, the Brackenburn clinic holds drop-in sessions that anyone can attend. These involve a short presentation at 4pm (and again at 5pm). The sessions are aimed at people considering seeking a referral, or those on the waiting list for an appointment. Referrals can be made by a patient's GP, or other supporting practitioners (such as local mental health teams). Referrals can be sent by post or email. There is no formal referral form, and so a referral should simply include basic information such as the service user's physical and mental health history, and any current medication.

Chapter 5

Care Separate from Transition

Like any other patients, most healthcare that trans people will need over their lives will have nothing to do with their gender. This is most obviously the case with the most common ailments we might associate with primary care – the problems that we most likely take to General Practitioners. Other primary care professionals include nurse practitioners, pharmacists, dental practitioners, and optometrists. Such practitioners will primarily benefit from respectful use of language and an understanding of trans people (as addressed in Chapters 1 and 2). However, this chapter will include specific considerations when providing for trans patients, *other* than making referrals to GICs (see Chapter 4, or Chapter 6 for children and adolescents), prescribing or managing hormone regimens (Chapter 7), or any aftercare related to gender-affirming surgeries (Chapter 8).

Secondary and tertiary medical practice unrelated to transition is also the subject of this chapter. Secondary care services are specialised sub-disciplines of medicine, consultant-led, and often delivered in the context of a hospital. Acute care, such as outpatient surgery centres, or Accident and Emergency (AandE) departments[1] are also forms of secondary care. Tertiary care is also specialised, but associated with separate centres, with particular facilities or equipment, for instance to perform specialised surgeries. In these

---

1   Variously known as emergency departments/wards/centres/rooms (ERs), or 'casualty', depending on the country of context.

more specialist contexts, sexual dimorphism[2] may be relevant in the provision of care.

Little has been written on any specific needs a trans person might have in relation to specialist practice that does not form part of a medical transition[3]. Whenever gender necessitates differences in individual medical care, this will be relevant to the treatment of trans patients. Likewise, if a doctor takes gender into account when making particular diagnoses or not, due to differences in risk (e.g. breast cancer in women versus men), this may also need to consider trans status, or any health interventions a trans person has had in relation to gender.

It is always vital to be mindful, respectful, and validating of a patient's gender. Therefore, in this chapter, discussions of medical treatment are specifically about the prescription of drugs and their dosages, physical examination techniques, interpretation of test results, and so forth, rather than the interpersonal dimensions of healthcare – which are relevant for all practitioners.

This chapter begins by highlighting the complex differences in risks and needs seen between cisgender men and cisgender women. This allows for the consideration of when a trans person's healthcare needs may be similar to, or different from, the gender they were assigned at birth. This is followed by a discussion of primary care, which due to the extreme variation of general practice is inevitably not exhaustive.

Secondary and tertiary considerations are then collectively considered, and are organised alphabetically by medical sub-field. Clearly, the practice of medicine does not always easily or neatly cut along discipline lines. Further, these discussions are severely limited by a lack of trans-specific research, and rely primarily on reinterpretation or application of research that has considered the intersections of (cisgender) 'men's/women's health' in relation to specialist practice.

---

2 Physiological differentiation between men and women that is understood as 'sexed', but other than the genitals and gonads.

3 With the notable exceptions of mental and sexual health – yet the impact such work has had across medical practice has been limited and inconsistent, and much work remains to be done.

Health disparities between cisgender men and cisgender women

It is well recognised that gender assignment at birth is linked to health disparities, as illustrated (non-exhaustively) in the table below:

Table 5.1: Health issues associated with cisgender status

Associated with cisgender men	Associated with cisgender women
Andrological health (prostate, testes, etc.)	Gynaecological health (uterus, ovaries, cervix, etc.)
Hematologic malignancies	Breast cancer
Cardiovascular disease	Complications of childbirth
Abdominal aortic aneurysms	Alzheimer's and vascular dementia
X-chromosome linked genetic conditions	Osteoporosis
Unintentional accidents and injuries	Autoimmune diseases
Autism (controversial biological/social intersection)	Physical and emotional harm related to domestic or sexual violence
Some psychological conditions (substance abuse disorders, antisocial personality disorder, etc.)	Some psychological conditions (borderline, and histrionic personality disorders, etc.)

The table considers *cisgender* men and women, as these are the gendered groups with which health research has been conducted. Many of these health concerns involve an intersection between biology and behaviour. For example, iron deficiency anaemia can be connected to menstruation, have a dietary cause, and/or be linked to parasitic infection. Therefore, biology and environment (social and geographical) may all be implicated to greater, lesser, or no extent in each individual case. This also illustrates how a single condition may have multiple different causes. As another example, the causes of postpartum depression (PPD) are not well understood, but is seen in both cisgender women and cisgender men. If the biological changes experienced during pregnancy are implicated in PPD for cisgender women (Bloch *et al.* 2003), then differential processes must be at play in cisgender men.

Gendered associations with conditions can result in neglecting less common, but clearly very real cases – vascular dementia, breast cancer, eating disorders, etc. in cisgender men, or X-chromosome linked genetic conditions, anger management problems (intermittent explosive disorder), autism, etc. in cisgender women.

Being trans may result in changes to some gender-related risks, but not to others, depending on whether gender affirming medical interventions are accessed, and if so, which. For example, a trans woman is most likely[4] to have an XY chromosomal makeup, opening the possibility of circumstances that might defy a practitioner's expectations, such as a woman presenting with haemophilia. Further, if someone has 'male' on their patient records, breast cancer becomes a much more likely and thus important consideration if they are someone AMAB taking estrogen, or someone AFAB who has changed the record of their gender but not accessed top surgery[5] (a common term for any gender affirming surgery of the chest area, such as mastectomy).

Not only is patient behaviour important to consider, but so is the social behaviour and beliefs of doctors and researchers. Unconscious gender biases and the unavoidable impact of socialisation can shape diagnoses and research methodologies. This has been a key discussion in research and practice on autism (Fine 2010, Jarrold and Brock 2004). Whilst autism is believed to be more common in cis men than cis women, this may be due to under-diagnosis in cis women, and/or flawed theorisation that has constructed autism as 'extreme maleness' (Baron-Cohen 2004, Fine 2010). Autism diagnoses have been found to correlate with gender non-conformity, notably, non-binary gender identities (Walsh *et al.* 2017). The hypotheses around this correlation are beyond the scope of this text; however, caution is advised against presuming that difficulties with social interaction (as with Asperger Syndrome) is resultant or causative of 'gender confusion'. An alternative hypothesis is that the unintelligibility of socially constructed gender roles renders the autistic individual with greater acuity of their internal sense of self.

---

4   Not absolutely certain, due to the possibility of asymptomatic sex chromosome variation being present – as is also true for the cisgender population.

5   It is worth noting here that not all breast tissue is removed during chest reconstruction for AFAB trans people.

In addition, there are complexities around the relationship between gender and health concerns – women are more likely to attempt suicide because of depression, but male suicide attempts are more likely to be successful. It is too simple to say one group experiences depression 'more' than the other, as this does not consider severity, or gendered under-reporting. Under-reporting by men is a large problem across all healthcare, due to pressures against 'showing weakness' in relation to a masculine identity, such that overall, men are less likely to make medical appointments and more likely to downplay symptoms. In many parts of the world, gender roles differentiate participation in the labour force, or at least the types of jobs people have, and therefore associated risks of injury, etc.

The trans population is extremely varied. Whether a person is taking hormones or has received gender affirming surgical interventions may be relevant to healthcare needs that are entirely unrelated to their gender affirming medical interventions themselves. Additionally, patients may have a sex marker on their medical records that does not reflect their physiological make-up. The table below illustrates these differences, all of which may need subtle differences in care:

Table 5.2: Circumstances of different trans people presenting for care

Gender of trans patient	Assignment at birth	Gender marker on medical records	Prescribed hormones?	Received surgeries?
Female	Male	F	No	No
Female	Male	F	Yes	No
Female	Male	F	No	Yes
Female	Male	F	Yes	Yes
Female	Male	M	No	No
Female	Male	M	Yes	No
Female	Male	M	No	Yes
Female	Male	M	Yes	Yes
Male	Female	F	No	No
Male	Female	F	Yes	No
Male	Female	F	No	Yes
Male	Female	F	Yes	Yes

Gender of trans patient	Assignment at birth	Gender marker on medical records	Prescribed hormones?	Received surgeries?
Male	Female	M	No	No
Male	Female	M	Yes	No
Male	Female	M	No	Yes
Male	Female	M	Yes	Yes
Non-Binary	Male	F	No	No
Non-Binary	Male	F	Yes	No
Non-Binary	Male	F	No	Yes
Non-Binary	Male	F	Yes	Yes
Non-Binary	Male	M	No	No
Non-Binary	Male	M	Yes	No
Non-Binary	Male	M	No	Yes
Non-Binary	Male	M	Yes	Yes
Non-Binary	Female	F	No	No
Non-Binary	Female	F	Yes	No
Non-Binary	Female	F	No	Yes
Non-Binary	Female	F	Yes	Yes
Non-Binary	Female	M	No	No
Non-Binary	Female	M	Yes	No
Non-Binary	Female	M	No	Yes
Non-Binary	Female	M	Yes	Yes

This table is limited in its modelling of the circumstances of different trans people. Most critically, how long a person has been on hormones is highly relevant – the impact on the body from one month on testosterone versus ten years, for instance, cannot be conflated. Further, there are very many different surgical procedures that may be accessed. In terms of frequency, some of the possible combinations above are much more likely than others – if someone has accessed hormones and surgery for example, it is very unlikely that they have not arranged for their gender marker to have been altered on their medical records. It is also more common for trans people to access hormones before surgery, however surgery before (or without) hormones is increasingly being recognised as an entirely valid transition pathway choice.

There are still many unknowns regarding the specifics of trans healthcare. For example, it is known that hepatocellular carcinoma is more common in cisgender men than cisgender women (Naugler *et al.* 2007). Is this related to hormone profile, in which case should we expect AMAB trans people taking estrogen and AFAB trans people taking testosterone to have risk similar to cisgender women, and men respectively? In trying to produce best practice for trans patients, there are three questions that need to be asked:

- When is it appropriate for a healthcare intervention to be similar or the same as those who were assigned the same way at birth (i.e. for a trans woman or AMAB non-binary person to receive similar treatment to a cisgender man, and for a trans man or an AFAB non-binary to receive similar treatment to a cisgender woman)?

- When is it appropriate for a healthcare intervention to be similar or the same as cisgender people with the same gender (i.e. for a trans woman to receive the same treatment as a cisgender woman, and for a trans man to receive the same treatment as a cisgender man)?

- When is gender irrelevant in healthcare treatment?

In many contexts, gender affirming medical interventions – hormones and surgeries – mean that a trans patient's health needs are the same as cisgender people of the same gender. That is, treatment of a trans woman is the same as a cisgender woman, and treatment of a trans man is the same as a cisgender man. Of course, the treatment of men and women is also often very similar or identical – such as a broken bone, or tonsillitis.

There has been very little specific research done to address non-transition related specialist healthcare in trans people. Therefore, the medical literature which considers the role of gender difference in different medical specialisations must be interpreted with caution to establish if, and when, special consideration is needed for a trans patient. For all secondary and tertiary practitioners, the information on language and communication (Chapters 1, 2, and 3) are all relevant, and all practitioners should remember to avoid assuming all their patients are cisgender, as medical records may not provide 'clues' such as a gendered name that does not 'match' gender designation and/or gendered title, hormone prescriptions, or records of surgery. There is a literature that examines sex/gender difference across different aspects of clinical medicine (Oertelt-Prigione and Regitz-Zagrosek 2011), however, given that some of the authors working in this area are still finding it necessary to answer the question 'do I really need to study females?' (Greenspan *et al.* 2007, p.S26), it is no surprise that trans men, women, and non-binary people are completely unrecognised.

Giving extended accounts in relation to all sub-specialties of medicine is clearly beyond the scope of this chapter, therefore it is strongly recommended that readers delve into the cited references for additional information. Further, where a given specialty is not highlighted (such as ophthalmology, respiratory medicine, neurology, etc.) there is either no significant gender differentiation (such that understanding of sensitive language, administration, and individual circumstances are adequate), gender difference has been conceived in terms of behavioural differences that cannot be applied in the consideration of an individual patient (rather than physiologically differentiating factors), or there is a lack of even speculative research.

Discussion of risk in relation to hormone replacement therapies will be addressed in more detail within Chapter 7. It is important for clinicians to recognise the medical necessity of hormones for trans people who report the experience of dysphoria. Patients need to be aware of associated risks, however (with the exceptions of absolute contraindications, which are very few) concern over *potential* risk or side-effects does not *automatically* justify a clinician denying or ceasing hormone access. If an intersecting concern presents in a given case, this should be discussed with the trans person and other relevant specialists as necessary to establish how they would wish to proceed, because of the potentially extreme risks that ceasing or denying HRT (hormone replacement therapy) can produce. In rare cases where a risk:benefit ratio is concluded to deny hormone access, clinicians should look for other ways that masculinisation or feminization may be medically pursued using different agents (e.g. inability to take estrogen does not contraindicate antiandrogens). Clinicians should also take into account if a patient declares they will self-medicate with hormones against medical advice, as providing access to a reputable source and blood monitoring may be justified under a principle of harm reduction.

Primary care unrelated to trans status

It is clearly not feasible to examine the enormity of possibilities that patients may present with in a primary care context. Many healthcare concerns which require referral to secondary care providers will be initially encountered by GPs, and so familiarity with the discussions that form the rest of this chapter are pertinent.

Due to the struggle with dysphoria relating to the body that many trans people face, primary care practitioners should be mindful about how physical examinations may be experienced, if required for concerns such as breast lumps, growth of moles, or rashes. Regardless of the individual relationship with social transition or pre-, post-, or non-surgical status, a given trans person may prefer a clinician of their own gender to perform an examination. Inquire if there is any way to minimise any distress that may be associated with such a check, including how intimate parts of the body may be differentially referred to (chest rather than breast, etc.).

It has also been recognised that nursing curricula do not prepare nurses in the provision of trans-sensitive or specific practices. Recent revisions of some teaching curricula have been made (McDowell and Bower 2016), and it remains important for working environments to be trans inclusive, and for cisgender nurse practitioners to recognise the possibility of gender diversity among colleagues (Cicero and Black 2016, Levesque 2015). This is a point that should be generalised beyond nurses, to all practitioners recognising the possibility of trans colleagues.

Secondary and tertiary care

Allergology

Allergology is the study of allergies and hypersensitivity reactions. It has been established that rates of atopy (assessed via skin test reactivity testing) are lower in cisgender girls than in cisgender boys until at least the age of 15, up until their early-to-mid 20s (DunnGalvin *et al.* 2006), yet is reversed in adulthood (Chen *et al.* 2008, Choi 2011). The mechanism by which such a reversal occurs is not entirely understood (Nicolai *et al.* 2003), however, sex steroids have an impact on autoimmunity, with Da Silva noting that 'Globally, estrogens depress T cell-dependent immune function and diseases, but enhance antibody production and aggravate B cell-dependent diseases. Androgens suppress both T-cell and B-cell immune responses and virtually always result in the suppression of disease expression' (Da Silva 1999, p.102). In the context of allergies therefore, a trans person's hormone profile is relevant as 'testosterone is an immunosuppressant and is likely to be protective, while [estrogens] are proinflammatory and will increase the susceptibility to atopy' (Osman 2003, p.587).

As a result, there is potential for conditions such as asthma to be slightly exacerbated for people who take estrogen-based HRT. This is not a reason for HRT to be denied or stopped, but simply an association with an estrogen-oriented hormone profile. Conversely, trans people who access testosterone HRT may experience a reduction in allergic symptoms.

Anaesthesiology

The use of anaesthesia to reduce or relieve pain, and/or induce temporary loss of sensation or consciousness (in perioperative medicine by an anaesthesiologist or an intensivist) includes gender as a factor when calculating risk – Pleym *et al.* note that 'gender should be taken into account as a factor that may be predictive for the dosage of several anesthetic drugs' (2003, p.241). This is related to body fat percentage, which is affected by hormone profile. Important gendered factors are cardiac output, which is relevant in the clearance of many intravenous anaesthetics, and CYP enzymatic activity for low-extraction drugs (Pleym *et al.* 2003). Use of oral contraceptives can alter CYP enzyme activity, which may be relevant for trans men and AFAB non-binary people.

Additionally, gendered differences to particular anaesthetics have been demonstrated. For example, cisgender women wake up faster than cisgender men when the drug propofol is used, due to a faster decline in plasma propofol – possibly due to gendered pharmacokinetics (Hoymork and Raeder 2005). In another context, cisgender women have been shown to be more susceptible to the neuromuscular blocker rocuronium, but not cisatracurium (Adamus *et al.* 2008). The differential responses to such drugs are not well understood. Future trans-inclusive research is necessary.

Trans people receiving estrogen HRT are required to stop their hormone regimen prior to surgery. It has been established that cisgender women taking HRT have a three- to four-fold increase in the relative risk of venous thromboembolism – a blood clot in a vein (Brighouse 2001). Temporary suspension of estrogen for four to six weeks prior to surgery has been recommended (NHS England 2007). Use of spironolactone (which reduces plasma testosterone levels) may also need to be put on hold, as it has a hypotensive effect (reduces blood pressure) – which may interfere with the response of the administering of vasopressors (given to raise blood pressure).

Cardiology

A recent academic review has considered the evidence for potential interplay between HRT in trans people and cardiovascular disease (Streed *et al.* 2017). It was found that 'CVD [cardiovascular disease] risk is largely unchanged among trans men receiving CSHT [cross-sex hormone therapy] compared with either cisgender women or cisgender men not receiving exogenous hormones' (Streed *et al.* 2017, p.3). It is summarised that while there are no increases in cardiovascular morbidity or mortality, trans men and AFAB non-binary people taking testosterone may be at greater risk of increased blood pressure, insulin resistance, or lipid derangements.

People assigned male at birth are at higher risk of Abdominal Aortic Aneurysm (AAA). This is not mitigated for trans women and non-binary people who were assigned male at birth through hormones or surgeries. Likewise, the risk for trans men and AFAB non-binary people remains lower for AAA. Screening invitations are sent to all individuals who are over the age of 65, and registered as male with their GP. Trans men are still welcome to access screening if they wish despite lower risk. Trans women registered as female are not currently routinely invited – a flaw of the current administration system. Practitioners should arrange for any transfeminine patients over the age of 65 to be sent invitations for AAA screening. This involves an ultrasound of the abdomen, and does not require the patient to undress completely (but to lift one's top layers).

Estrogen-based HRT for trans women is associated with thromboembolic risk (Shatzel *et al.* 2017). This has resulted in lower dose transdermal and oral bioidentical estrogen being preferable to high-dose oral ethinyl estradiol formulations (Streed *et al.* 2017). A study that looked at the prevalence of myocardial infarction among 214 trans women with an average age of 44, receiving hormones for an average of 7.4 years, found an incidence higher than a control group of cisgender women (of whom 30% were receiving HRT). Prevalence among the trans women cohort was similar to cisgender men not receiving exogenous hormones (Wierckx *et al.* 2013).

Dermatology

Trans people may have specific needs from a dermatologist, as 'exogenous hormones affect hair and sebum production, gender-confirming surgeries often require dermatologic pre- and postoperative interventions, and postoperative anatomy may show unique presentations of routine skin conditions' (Ginsberg 2016, p.65). Estrogen will quickly and persistently reduce sebum (skin oil) production (Giltay and Gooren 2000), potentially causing dry skin (xerosis) for some.

Trans men and AFAB non-binary people who take testosterone may experience severe acne (Turrion-Merino *et al.* 2015, Wierckx *et al.* 2014). Dermatologists should be mindful if an AFAB trans person with a possibility of pregnancy requires isotretinoin as a form of treatment, because this may cause congenital disorders (Rieder *et al.* 2016). Testosterone HRT may also result in male-pattern baldness, which in the context of a trans patient may require different treatment. Ginsberg notes that while topical minoxidil is unlikely to have any interactions with hormones, it remains 'unclear whether patients would require the standard 1 mg dosage similar to their cisgender male counterparts or the 5 mg dosing that is often necessary for cisgender women with androgenetic alopecia' (Ginsberg 2016, p.66). It is also warned that finasteride not be given to trans people taking testosterone until two years or more after beginning HRT, because this may otherwise block the development of hormone-associated developments.

Endocrinology

Endocrinological management of HRT dominates the discussion of trans endocrinology, which is addressed in Chapter 7. The safety of HRT for trans people has been established (Gooren *et al.* 2008, Weinand and Safer 2015), even without consideration of the risks of non-treatment. In a United States context, it was found that while almost 80 per cent of endocrinologists had treated a trans patient, 80.6 per cent had never received trans-specific training (Davidge-Pitts *et al.* 2017).

With regards to prevalent endocrinological health concerns that may present in trans people as with cisgender people (such as diabetes, or thyroid disease) there is limited research. The 7th edition of the WPATH (World Professional Association for Transgender Health) Standards of Care indicates a possibility of increased risk of type II diabetes when receiving estrogen HRT, particularly with a family history or other risk factors present. Diabetes does not exclude a trans person from surgeries, but as for a cisgender diabetic needing surgery, coordination between the surgeon and managing practitioner is recommended (Ellsworth and Colon 2006).

It has been noted that if a patient has been prescribed 'thyroxin replacement for hypothyroidism, it is important to monitor TSH and free T4 closely as testosterone can affect thyroid binding globulin' (James 2013, p.8). While specific research is needed, this is a consideration for trans patients taking testosterone if diagnosed with hypothyroidism.

Gastroenterology

While more detail will be given in Chapter 8, one method of vaginoplasty used is total laparoscopic sigmoid vaginoplasty, which uses colonic segments as pedicled grafts. This should be followed up with vaginoscopy by a gastroenterologist (Bouman 2016).

Gender differences have been studied in relation to Irritable Bowel Syndrome (IBS), and gastrointestinal pain (Mayer *et al.* 2004, Shiotani *et al.* 2006). People assigned male at birth less commonly experience mucus, incomplete evacuation, distension and scybala (hardened faecal mass), meaning the Manning and Rome criteria are less reliable in the diagnosis of IBS for people assigned male at birth (Thompson 1997). Additionally, there has been some research investigating why oesophageal and gastric adenocarcinoma are found more frequently in individuals assigned male at birth (Rutegård *et al.* 2010). Due to the decrease in the gap between male and female diagnoses with age, it has been hypothesised that premenopausal estrogen may be protective of non-cardia gastric adenocarcinoma – but no trans-specific research has been done and there is a lack of conclusive evidence.

Geriatrics

A small body of specific literature has been produced which considers the intersection between age, healthcare, and trans status – although much of this is (importantly) focused around social stigma and discrimination (American Geriatrics Society Ethics Committee 2015, Donovan 2001, Persson 2009, Porter *et al.* 2016, Siverskog 2014). While there is a significant absence of long-term healthcare studies of trans people into later life, transgender cultural competency is likely the most important additional knowledge needed in the care of older trans people.

Haematology/blood tests

Haematologists should bear in mind that a patient's trans status may explain otherwise unexpected blood test results. For example, anaemia (iron deficiency) is considerably more common in people assigned female at birth, and higher still in people who menstruate (Schmetzer and Flörcken 2011) – which includes some trans men and AFAB non-binary people. Schmetzer and Flörcken state that 'we are still at the beginning [of understanding] the influence of gene polymorphisms, epigenetic changes, dietary effects, environmental factors, and immune system differences between the sexes. At least it is now clear that all these play important roles; however years of research are needed to draw a first picture' (2011, p.152).

HRT will shift blood test results in addition to the hormonal concentrations – testosterone for example, raises red blood cell count (polycythaemia), and increases haemoglobin and haematocrit (Kandhro 2016). Further discussion of HRT can be found in Chapter 7.

Hospital wards/surgery

The 'Transgender Guide for NHS Acute Hospital Trusts'[6] is aimed to support frontline hospital staff, as well as directors and board members. It is particularly important that staff are familiar with the protections given by the Gender Recognition Act. A person's trans status is *protected information*, meaning it is illegal for this information to be shared or revealed. The right to non-disclosure is maintained in death. Where medically necessary to inform another practitioner of a patient's trans status, explicit consent must be gained. Familiarity with the rights trans people have to confidentiality is particularly necessary for an institution's Caldicott Guardian[7] (a senior staff member responsible for the protection of patient confidentiality). Trans people may refuse to disclose any or all parts of their medical data, even where practitioners may believe this is not in their best medical interest.

Same-sex accommodation (in ward settings, for example) for trans patients should be provided in alignment with the trans person's identity. Staff *may not* use the following factors to deny access to same-sex accommodation:

- not 'looking enough like' a woman (for a trans woman to be on a women's ward) or a man (for a trans man to be on a man's ward)

- the clothing someone chooses to wear (e.g. a trans woman wearing trousers)

- whether a person has changed their name by deed poll or on NHS records

---

6 By Royal Free Hampstead NHS Trust, and available for download here (accessed 10/08/2017): uktrans.info/attachments/article/5/trasngender_booklet_low%20res.pdf

7 The Caldicott Principles state that any purpose for using confidential information must be justified, it may only be used when absolutely necessary, only the minimum amount of information required may be used, access is on a need-to-know basis, and all staff must understand their responsibilities and comply with the law.

- whether a person has accessed hormones

- whether a person has accessed gender-affirming surgery/ surgeries

- whether a person has a Gender Recognition Certificate (GRC).

It is reasonable to use a patient's overall intended gender presentation to infer gender identity – and this may be necessary in a context where a patient is unconscious or incapacitated upon admission. If a patient is androgynous or non-binary, it is appropriate to respectfully ask which ward would be preferable. In some cases, a trans person may wish to be placed on a ward for the gender they were assigned at birth. This may be the case for some non-binary people, or for a trans man or woman who is newly out and yet to change their name, pronouns, or presentation. However, in such a case, it is very unlikely that the person would disclose that they are trans, and would simply bear with an uncomfortably gendered situation. Thus, it remains important to avoid making assumptions about anyone's gender, even in the context of a gendered ward.

Differences in the appearances of intimate areas is never a bar to inclusion in a same-sex ward, as bed curtains provide privacy. If possible, accommodation in a single side-room adjacent to a gender-appropriate ward may be a solution that mitigates anxiety in the trans patient. In cases where another patient may act or speak in a derogatory way to a trans patient, staff may need to reinforce their institution's zero tolerance to discrimination policy – without 'outing' a patient as trans. If a situation arises where views of family members differ from a trans patient's, the trans person's view is given priority.

It is common for a trans person's gender marker on their medical records to be updated to match their identity prior to, or without, accessing surgery. If a trans patient is in hospital for an unrelated surgery, their trans status may or may not be relevant. If trans status is not disclosed and not relevant (for example, bunion removal) surgeons may not view this as a 'deception' or an omission that justifies a refusal to operate – this would be a breach of the Equality Act (refusal of treatment because of trans status). In other cases, surgeons may benefit from knowing the internal physiology of a patient prior to even unrelated surgeries (such as appendectomy).

Mental health

Mental health is particularly complex in the context of trans healthcare, because of the impact of minority stress (Gamarel *et al.* 2014, Hendricks and Testa 2012, Kelleher 2009) and micro-aggressions (Chang and Chung 2015). For information on trans-affirmative therapeutic interactions, please refer to Chapter 3. Evidence suggests that being trans is not linked to, or part of any psychopathological disorder (Cole *et al.* 1997, Hoshiai *et al.* 2010). Very few case studies exist that look at serious mental illness (outside of depression and anxiety) within the trans population (Garrett 2004).

There has been a small recognition of the potential for disordered eating to be connected to an individual's experience of gender dysphoria, whereby striving for thinness can be an attempt to suppress secondary sexual characteristics associated with assignment at birth, such as fat distribution or breast growth (Ålgars *et al.* 2012). In such co-presentation (as with anxiety and depression) effective assistance with any desired transition process may strongly synergise in alleviating such other issues (Strandjord *et al.* 2015).

Mental health difficulties not necessarily connected to experiences of stress, stigma, and discrimination are likely to occur at similar frequencies to the overall population. The 2012 Trans Mental Health Survey (McNeil *et al.* 2012) found that 621 people (66% of respondents) had used mental health services for reasons other than to access assistance with gender reassignment. Recent research within trans youth has suggested that 'socially transitioned transgender children who are supported in their gender identity have developmentally normative levels of depression and only minimal elevations in anxiety, suggesting that psychopathology is not inevitable within this group' (Olson *et al.* 2016, p.1).

Nephrology

On average, people assigned female at birth have a lower number of nephrons in their kidneys (Regitz-Zagrosek 2012). It has been found that cis women have more stage three chronic kidney diseases than cis men, yet lupus nephritis and polycystic kidney disease are more common in cis men (Gallieni 2012, Silbiger and Neugarten 2008). Differential development may therefore mean that risks for AMAB trans people is similar to cisgender men, and the risk for AFAB trans people is similar to cisgender women, but no specific research has been conducted.

A clear demonstration of how transphobic social policy may influence transgender *kidney* health indirectly is the case of bathroom-related discrimination. Schuster *et al.* (2016, p.101) explain that:

> Transgender people who are barred from using bathrooms where they feel safe might feel they have no choice but to suppress basic bodily needs. Delayed bathroom use can cause health problems including urinary tract or kidney infections, stool impaction, and haemorrhoids. Some transgender people even abstain from drinking during the day to avoid the need to urinate.

While in a UK context trans people are theoretically protected by the Equality Act 2010, many trans people still report venues which police or restrict toilet access. Further, non-binary people may be unsafe or feel dysphoric using male or female toilets, lending additional credence to arguments for gender-neutral bathroom spaces (Erickson-Schroth and Jacobs 2017). There exists no evidence that trans people pose a 'threat' to other public bathroom users, whilst being at considerable risk of verbal, physical, or sexual assault themselves regardless of bathroom choice (Seelman 2014).

Obstetrics and gynaecology

This branch of medicine is highly pertinent for most AFAB trans people, but also for AMAB trans people who have received vaginoplasty. The importance of gynaecological care is beginning to be recognised for trans people (Dutton *et al.* 2008, Obedin-Maliver 2015, van Trotsenburg 2009, Weyers *et al.* 2010). Public Health England have released a pamphlet, 'Information for trans people' on NHS Screening Programmes (Public Health England 2017). This includes information related to breast, cervical, abdominal aortic aneurysm, and bowel screening. A hyperlink to where the pamphlet can be downloaded is found in the references list.

The prostate is not removed during vaginoplasty, therefore trans women may remain at risk of prostate cancer regardless of transition pathway or none. Decreased testosterone levels (in trans women and AMAB non-binary people who have the testicles removed, or take testosterone blockers) lowers the risk of prostate cancer, but cannot eliminate it completely. Transvaginal (through the vagina) palpitation and ultrasound are possibilities that should be considered by gynaecologists and radiologists (Miksad *et al.* 2006). Weyers *et al.* (2009) found that in a cohort of fifty trans women, transvaginal prostate palpitation was possible for 48 per cent, and the prostate was visible on transvaginal ultrasound for 94 per cent. These methods of examination may be easier or more comfortable for some trans women over rectal examination.

Trans women and non-binary people who were assigned male at birth do not require cervical screening. If registered as female with their GP, such patients will still receive cervical screening invitations due to the oversimplifying nature of the current automated system – these invitations can be ignored, yet practitioners should update their records to prevent unnecessary invitations. Trans men or non-binary people assigned female at birth are eligible for cervical screening – unless having received a total hysterectomy, whereby the cervix is also removed. Trans men and AFAB non-binary people who are registered with their GP as male will not receive invitations for screening, which thus requires individuals to ask for a test. Practitioners should recognise that this may be particularly difficult or distressing, and can also set up invitations/reminders associated with the patient record for those aged between 25 and 64. Trans men and AFAB non-binary people who are registered with their GP as female will receive invitations. Human Papilloma Virus (HPV) is strongly associated with cervical cancer, emphasising the importance of inclusive sexual health screening practices for the health of the trans male community.

As with the general population, many trans people wish or plan to become parents. Due to the sterilising effects of some gender-affirming surgeries and the impact on fertility of HRT, cryopreservation can be performed of oocytes, ovarian tissue, sperm, testicular tissue, or embryos, as can surgical sperm extraction (De Roo *et al.* 2016, Mitu 2016). Trans male pregnancy is also becoming increasingly recognised. Desire for, or ambivalence towards pregnancy does not exclude someone from being male, and/or from not being female. Physicians must understand that being trans does not eliminate one from being a parent, and being a parent does not eliminate one from medically assisted transition, while also being familiar with the impact that different interventions may have on fertility.

As discussed in the dermatology subsection, prescription of isotretinoin (or any medication that may cause birth defects) must not be given to any trans man or AFAB non-binary person attempting to become pregnant (Yeung *et al.* 2016). Significant numbers of men (and non-binary people) have used testosterone prior to pregnancy (Light *et al.* 2014), however stopping testosterone HRT prior to conception is necessary. Light *et al.*'s study reported that most (20 out of 25) who had used testosterone resumed menstruation within 6 months of stopping (and most within three months), indicating testosterone HRT does not necessarily cause irreversible cessation of menstruation (amenorrhoea) – despite this being previously reported (T'Sjoen *et al.* 2013). Five people among Light *et al.*'s respondents reported conception prior to the return of menstruation.

Obstetricians should be equipped with trans-sensitive language that takes account of individual circumstances. This not only includes the trans person's pronouns (as in all healthcare settings), but whether they would wish to be referred to as father/parent rather than 'mother', or plans regarding chest feeding and potential resumption or initiation of testosterone. Trans men may also be at greater risk of peripartum or postpartum depression, which may intersect with experiences of dysphoria.

Oncology

The study of gender differences in cancer susceptibility has been reviewed, concluding that cisgender men have a higher overall risk of cancer than cisgender women, and that some of the most common cancers (colorectal, lung, non-Hodgkin lymphoma, and bladder) have the sharpest gendered ratios with more cis men diagnosed (Dorak and Karpuzoglu 2012). Cancer of the breast, gall bladder, anus, and thyroid have higher incidences in cis women (Cook *et al.* 2009).

Cancer in trans people raises two factors for consideration – which forms of cancer have risks that stay the same with assignment at birth, and can risk alter with transition (such that a trans woman's risk of a particular type of cancer is the same as a cis woman's, for instance)? A large-scale study has investigated the incidence of breast cancer in 5,135 trans people (Brown and Jones 2015). Of this cohort, ten cases of breast cancer were found, seven in people assigned female at birth, and three in people assigned male at birth. A separate study (Gooren *et al.* 2013) which included 2,307 trans women and 795 trans men, all of whom received HRT (estrogen or testosterone, respectively) found the incidences of breast cancer in both groups similar to the expected incidence for cis men.

It is therefore believed that trans people's risk of breast cancer is not increased using HRT (estrogen or testosterone based). The decrease in risk seen for trans men compared to cisgender women may be due to the commonality of mastectomy within this group. Any individual with breast tissue has some level of risk. In very rare cases this has included trans men after bilateral mastectomy (Nikolic *et al.* 2012), and specific cases of trans women developing breast cancer have been studied (Dhand and Dhaliwal 2010). The 7th edition of the World Professional Association for Transgender Health Standards of Care specifies that family history of breast cancer, obesity, and the use of progestins may increase risk.

Cervical cancer/screening is discussed under 'obstetrics and gynaecology'. A case study reporting of two ovarian cancer cases in trans men has been used to argue that salpingo-oophorectomy (removal of ovaries and fallopian tubes) should be performed whenever a trans man accesses hysterectomy (Hage *et al.* 2000). However, more recent research reviewing the available literature and evidence found no strong evidence of increased risk of ovarian cancer in trans men, and no link between ovarian cancer development and taking testosterone (Harris *et al.* 2017).

There has been specific publication of a case of prostate cancer in a transgender woman, 41 years after accessing HRT (Miksad *et al.* 2006). In this case, oral bicalutamide and dutasteride were prescribed, which were effective in their antiandrogenic functions while also being maintainable with the patient's estrogen regimen. Indeed, bicalutamide may be an option as part of transfeminine HRT due to its antiandrogenic properties, such that synergy may be obtained in specific treatment circumstances. The impact of estrogen on prostate cancer is potentially complex, having been used as a treatment, but also implicated in development and progression (Nelles, Hu, and Prins 2011). AMAB trans people on estrogen may experience prostate shrinkage, which may make diagnosis by rectal examination alone difficult. The PSA (prostate specific antigen) test is an additional potential diagnostic tool.

Trans people's risk for many of the most gendered forms of cancer (breast, cervix, prostate) may be increased due to the avoidance of screening for such procedures due to the way these body parts are gendered creating a particularly stressful or dysphoria-inducing experience. Practitioners in both primary and secondary care settings should be proactive in the creation of affirming practices that are signposted effectively to the correct trans people who will benefit from them.

Sexual health/venereology

Practitioners should recognise that a trans person's gender identity does not provide any information about their sexual orientation, whether they have sex, and what kinds of sex they might have, if any. The context of sexual health also highlights the importance of not assuming genital configurations based on identity labels. For example, a trans woman who is a lesbian may have sex with a lesbian or bisexual woman who is cis, or trans. One, both, or neither of them may have a penis, so without more specific information it is not possible to know whether penis-in-vagina (PIV) or anal sex is occurring (or possible) within the context of a lesbian relationship/ sexual encounter.

While assumptions should never be made about any trans individual's sexual history, many trans people are at high risk of sexually transmitted infections (STIs). This is highly associated with high levels of stigma and discrimination which is linked to economic vulnerability, such that a comparably high proportion of the trans population, particularly trans women, may be sex workers, with especially high HIV risk (Nadal *et al.* 2014, Operario *et al.* 2008, Wilson *et al.* 2009). This does not mean, however, that a particular individual trans person is at high risk. If a trans person is at higher risk of HIV (e.g. has unprotected sex with gay/bisexual men) they may be eligible for PrEP (pre-exposure prophylaxis). PrEP offers protection against HIV but not other STIs.[8]

Some key points relevant for trans-specific sexual health:

- A person who appears male (e.g. a trans man or a non-binary person) may have need of emergency contraception, if they were assigned female at birth, and had vaginal sex without contraception (or where contraception has failed, such as a condom breaking). Emergency contraception should still be provided. Oral emergency contraception does not interfere with hormone therapy, and 'testosterone is not thought to affect efficacy of emergency hormonal contraception' (Royal College of Obstetricians and Gynaecologists 2017, p.3).

- For AFAB trans people, taking testosterone or gonadotropin releasing hormone (GnRH) analogues do not provide contraceptive protection.

- Combination hormonal contraception (which contain estrogen and progestogen) for AFAB trans people is not recommended if taking testosterone, as the estrogen present in these forms of contraception can interfere with the effectiveness of HRT. Progestogen-only contraception methods are not thought to interfere with hormone regimens.

- For AMAB trans people who are taking estradiol and are having vaginal sex (and have not received a vasectomy or orchidectomy), while estradiol lowers sperm count, it does not eliminate the possibility of pregnancy. Likewise, GnRH analogues or antiandrogens do not provide contraceptive protection.

The Faculty of Sexual and Reproductive Healthcare (FSRH) Clinical Effectiveness Unit (CEU) of the Royal College of Obstetricians and Gynaecologists released a statement on contraceptive choices for transgender people, in October 2017 (Royal College

---

8   For information on clinics participating in the provision of PrEP see: https://www.prepimpacttrial.org.uk/join-the-trial

of Obstetricians and Gynaecologists 2017). This provides specific guidance on contraception for binary-oriented and non-binary trans people, using appropriate language and taking into account specific nuances that may be relevant in providing trans-specific guidance and care.

In the context of the UK, there is currently a single sexual health service specific for trans people. This service, CliniQ, has been highly commended by the NHS as 'Inclusive Team of The Year 2016' and received the 2014 Nursing Times award for 'Enhancing Patient Dignity' (see the CliniQ website, cliniq.org.uk). The service is based in London, and is led by trans people. The organisation offers two-hour, half-day, and full-day training packages – see cliniq.org.uk/training for more information. In addition to sexual health services, CliniQ can also provide trans-sensitive smear tests, and can monitor blood levels for trans people who are self-medicating.[9]

Conclusion

An overarching theme in this chapter is the drastic lack of research done to provide guidance for treating trans people, where the medical interventions they may have accessed in relation to being trans may alter best practice. Feldman *et al.* (2016) highlight a need for more research into health disparities and comorbidity over the life span. Further, many of the research papers frame their studies as considering lesbian, gay, bisexual, and trans patients, and either conflate the needs of sexuality and gender identity minorities, or fail to engage in trans-specific analysis due to very small sample sizes. This chapter is inevitably limited, but aims to help the clinician to appreciate how, when, and why trans status may or may not impact the treatment for other medical needs, without assuming hormones or surgeries cannot or should not be accessed.

---

9   The service has created trans-specific sexual health literature, available here for AMAB trans people who have sex with AMAB people: cliniq.org.uk/resources/the-hook-up-a-trans-womans-guide-to-the-sex-club-scene   and here for AFAB trans people who have sex with AMAB people: cliniq.org.uk/resources/cruising-a-trans-guys-guide-to-the-gay-sex-scene

Chapter 6

Children and Adolescents

Few subjects have been reported by the mainstream media with as much sensationalism (and often, fabrication) as trans or gender-diverse young people. This chapter addresses the specific needs that are associated with gender diversity or trans identity in people under the age of eighteen. I use the phrase 'young people' to collectively refer to children and adolescents, and, in the context of children, I use 'trans' to include children with cross-gender identification even if not accompanied by specific identification with (or knowledge of) the term 'trans'. To ensure that discussions of support are not undermined, the chapter begins by unpacking and debunking misinformation which casts a shadow over the care and well-being of trans young people. This leads to an explanation of the importance of support, with further specific guidance for family, schools, and clinicians. The referral process is then explained – mirroring Chapter 4, by detailing policy at the clinics in England, Scotland, and Northern Ireland. Finally, this chapter goes into full detail about the role and use of puberty-blocking drugs, which can provide vital protection for young trans people, and prevent the development of gendered characteristics which could strongly heighten dysphoria.

Childhood and adolescence are periods of change and self-discovery. Unlike adult trans populations, children (in particular) are less likely to necessarily have a specific *transgender* identity, even in cases where (sometimes very young) children have an insistent, persistent, and consistent gender that differs from assignment at birth. As a result, this chapter makes greater use of the term 'gender difference', to indicate that some children who are referred to Gender Identity Services may defy traditional gender roles or expectations without necessarily having an unhappy relationship with their bodies, complex and evolving relationships with how gender is navigated socially, or even without disidentification from their assigned gender. Discussing young people in terms of gender difference allows this chapter's discussions to avoid implying that supporting gender identity or expression in young people necessarily depends on a self-conceptualisation as trans always being adopted. Of course, many young people who do not identify with their assignment at birth will and do conceive of themselves as trans, when this vocabulary and concept is available to them.

Vanderburgh (2009) found that 60.4 per cent of his trans male clients and 52.7 per cent of his trans female clients knew their gender identities prior to the age of five (Luecke 2011). Two important points can be drawn from this – firstly, regardless of the proportion of children expressing gender difference who socially and/or medically transition, many people who *do* transition had a strong sense of their genders from a young age, despite potential (or likelihood) of sociocultural factors which attempt to assert that their assigned sex is 'what they are'. Secondly, these numbers show that just because someone didn't express gender difference in childhood, this is not evidence that they are not trans. Personal circumstances and social environments mean there can be very large discrepancies between whether a person is able to honestly reflect upon and explore gender identity or not, and whether or not support is likely if someone feels they are not the gender they were assigned at birth. Gradual shifts in awareness, and increases in the number of people who are tolerant or accepting offer an intuitive and convincing explanation for the large increase seen in referrals to Gender Identity Services for young people. Young people are exploring and expressing their genders with more authenticity than ever before, yet there remain serious risks if support is not forthcoming.

Myths and misconceptions

Some of the most common allegations made about trans, gender diverse, and questioning children are that they are only 'confused', or 'mentally ill' (that the young person's feelings about gender are a result of being depressed, anxious, or suffering with PTSD). Some claim that gender diverse young people lack clearly gendered parental figures, that they have been influenced by an 'agenda' (of a parent or community), or that they're going through a phase, or following a trend (among friends, or wider social media). Such claims do not reflect the realities of trans, gender diverse, or questioning children and their families – yet the propagation of misinformation can strongly impact the wellbeing of children by delaying access to appropriate support.

'It's just a phase'? – desistance

'Desistance' and 'persistence' are controversial terms, and somewhat more frequent in research literature than in clinical practice, as they do not capture the complexity of outcomes. In short, desistance has been used to indicate people who have stopped experiencing gender dysphoria, and no longer consider themselves to be trans. In diagnostic terms, both the DSM and the ICD differentiate between a diagnosis of gender dysphoria in childhood, versus adolescence and adulthood. Steensma *et al.* have claimed their analysis of 10 studies – which collectively considered 246 children – showed persistent gender dysphoria in only 39 of them, giving a desistance figure of 84.2 per cent, varying between 73–98 per cent in the individual studies that were reviewed (Steensma *et al.* 2011). At first look, this would suggest it is reasonable to assume that children or adolescents who express a gender identity different to their assignment at birth are unlikely to maintain that identity long-term. However, the methodologies and analyses that underpin this claim are fundamentally flawed, also highlighting the vulnerability of clinical research to practitioner biases.

To calculate the percentage of young people who desist, one must have a sample comprised only of children with gender dysphoria, and subtract the number who continue to experience dysphoria in adolescence and adulthood (diagnostically, adolescence is grouped with adulthood, not with childhood). To produce their numerical claim, Steensma *et al.* draw from cohorts given in eight papers, and two books (only three of which were written within the last thirty years – one in 1995 and the other two in 2008 – over which time the conceptualisation of gender identity and sexuality have developed extensively). None of these pieces of work use cohorts only comprised of children with clear experiences of gender dysphoria. Three of the studies do not consider trans status or gender dysphoria at all, but rather were investigating the association between femininity in boys and sexuality (with a view to 'prevent' homosexuality). The samples of other studies are made up of children referred to gender identity clinics (remembering that no diagnosis needed to be made to access referral), many of whom were judged to be experiencing dysphoria at 'subclinical' thresholds. None of the studies made a clear distinction between gender dysphoric children, socially transitioned children, children diagnosed with 'Gender Identity Disorder' (GID, or other older terms used prior to Gender Dysphoria), or gender nonconforming children. Children could be diagnosed with GID without experiencing dysphoria, but when exhibiting gender nonconforming behaviours, or simply expressing a 'wish to be the opposite sex'. Because older diagnostic criteria were relied upon in all except two of the studies, there was no attention to the severity/constancy of gender dysphoria in childhood, such that many children were diagnosed with dysphoria with radically different experiences of disidentification with assignment at birth. As a result, Steensma *et al.*'s high desistance rate claim has been strongly challenged as an under-evidenced and unjustifiable claim (Winters 2014).

Winters (2014) has looked closely at both Steensma *et al.*'s (2011) research, and at two other influential studies (Drummond *et al.* 2008, Wallien and Cohen-Kettenis 2008) which also claim very high desistance rates – these are also the two most recently written papers reviewed out of the ten pieces considered by Steensma *et al.* in 2011. Drummond *et al.*'s (2008) work considered 25 AFAB people, 15 of whom met the criteria for GID in childhood (which could be met by gender non-conformity without dysphoria) and 10 of whom were 'subthreshold for the diagnosis'. Because only three individuals (12%) were later judged to have GID of adolescence or adulthood, a 'desistance' of 88 per cent was claimed. In Wallien and Cohen-Kettenis (2008), it was claimed that '27 per cent of our total group of gender dysphoric [sic] children was still gender dysphoric in adolescence'. The total group size was 77 children, however on follow-up, 23 of these children (30%) were unable to be contacted

– these children were assumed to have desisted. Of the contacted individuals, 39 per cent (21/54) were counted as 'persistent' in their gender dysphoria, which was dependent upon having applied for medical transition at the time when approached for follow-up. This therefore risked placing people with trans identities but who either had yet to access medical transition, people who felt able to address dysphoria with social transition only, and people who did not experience their gender in terms of distress but still did not identify with the gender assigned at birth – in the 'desistance' group. Additionally, as with Drummond *et al.*, the initial cohort likely contained many gender nonconforming children who had limited experiences of gender dysphoria. Tellingly, higher dysphoria scores in childhood were much better predictors of the need for medical transition in adolescence and adulthood. Recent peer-reviewed work has also identified significant methodological, theoretical, and interpretative problems with this earlier research (Newhook *et al.* 2018).

A diagnosis of gender dysphoria in childhood does not depend on the child expressing a need for later access to hormones or surgeries. As discussed elsewhere in the book, many trans people do not feel the need to access surgery (or even hormones), *yet all* of these studies would judge children who do not go on to access *medical* transitions as 'desisting'. Therefore, the 84 per cent figure is fundamentally flawed because the number of dysphoric children is not known, and it is also unknown how many continued to express a trans/gender diverse identity without medical transition in adolescence or adulthood. A follow-up study (Steensma *et al.* 2013) showed a strong relationship between the intensity of dysphoria experienced, and accessing gender-affirming medical interventions. Rather than conceiving young people as 'persisting' or 'desisting', clinicians may find it more helpful to consider three central factors for gender dysphoric children. Firstly, does a young person continue to meet diagnostic criteria for gender dysphoria as they move from childhood into adolescence? Secondly, how does the young person identify themselves? Finally, what desires, if any, does the young person have for physical interventions? Considering these questions allows for greater nuance, creating space to recognise that some young people who are trans do not require medical intervention in the management of gender dysphoria, but without labelling them as 'desisting' in their trans identity. This also keeps support available for those who require physical intervention to address gender dysphoria.

Parental influence?

As with sexuality, there is no evidence to support claims that differences in gender identity or expression are *caused* by parenting practices. The larger number of people that are seen accessing gender identity clinics (in both childhood and adulthood) is due to a gradual lessening of stigma and discrimination, such that more people feel able to express their experiences of gender without risking rejection. There is also an increasing awareness of the existence of medical and therapeutic support. This not only has the benefit of allowing children to explore their identities and access support where necessary, but also for cisgender children to engage in honest gender expression (clothing, activities, toy types) without this being taken as indicative of sexuality or gender identity in and of themselves.

Are trans children and adolescents mentally unwell?

For at least the last twenty years, it has been recognised that 'the argument that gross psychopathology is a required condition for the development of transsexualism [sic] appears indefensible' (Cohen *et al.* 1997). It has been demonstrated that for transgender children who have socially transitioned and are supported to live openly as their gender, no elevations in depression and only marginally higher anxiety is seen when compared to a control group (Olson *et al.* 2016). This strongly suggests that anxiety and depression in children are neither causative of, nor caused by, feelings of gender difference. Rather, rejection, stigma, and lack of support can result in these problems – which also may explain the marginally higher anxiety score, as there remains the risk of microaggressions or stigma from people outside of the child's family and friends. The higher risk of depression, anxiety, suicidal ideation or attempt, and self-harm that has been observed in trans adolescents is not symptomatic of trans identity or gender non-conformity, but the impact of cissexism and transphobia on well-being (Reisner *et al.* 2015).

This is not to imply that all trans young people who are depressed, anxious, or self-harm are/do so for the same or even similar reasons. It has been reported that 23 per cent of trans young people have engaged in self-harm (Di Ceglie *et al.* 2002), and it cannot be assumed all of these cases are a result of unsupportive environments. More recently, the Stonewall School Report (Stonewall 2017) reported that 84 per cent of trans young people have deliberately harmed themselves at some point[1]. Much of this is related to bullying or lack of support (the self-harm figure for LGB youth from the same source is 61%) but the specificity of some peoples' experiences of being trans may contribute. For example, gender dysphoria may manifest in an intense hatred of the body (or parts of the body) for some people, or experience a sense of betrayal at the body being 'wrong' relative to identity, such that self-harm may manifest as a direct attack on what is causing great distress (McNeil *et al.* 2012). In short, trans and gender diverse young people may be at greater risk of anxiety and depression if they are not accepted and supported, but there is nothing pathological about gender diversity itself. Despite this, the urgent need of physical intervention in the alleviation of distress may be necessary to mitigate self-harm for some trans young people.

Following the crowd?

This particular myth echoes 'concerns' expressed around non-heterosexual sexualities in adolescents (particularly bisexuality in girls). That is, people who reject identification with their assignment at birth can be accused of 'attention-seeking', or 'following a trend'. This is damaging for all youth, whether articulating a trans identity or not. Claiming that a person is 'simply' seeking attention or following a trend attempts to shame the young person about their

---

1   Readers may be curious about why there might be such a large difference between the figures given in the 2002 study, and the 2017 report. It is important to recognise that all participants in the 2002 study were recruited from a specialist gender identity development service, and were therefore much more likely to have parental and professional support in relation to gender identity, than respondents in the second data set.

self-expression, whether this is the intention or not. Even in cases where a young person's understanding of their gender identity or expression may change over time, it is important to recognise that there is nothing harmful about gender uncertainty, or gender fluidity. There is no evidence to suggest that cisgender youth are being 'confused by' and identifying erroneously as trans or gender non-conforming due to increased media recognition – particularly due to the fact that people cannot be 'turned trans'. This argument also typically involves the claim that being trans has become 'enticing', which entirely ignores the overwhelming extent to which gender non-conformity, gender difference, or being trans is still represented as undesirable or tragic (Serano 2007, Richardson 2016).

Alarmist claims appeal to notions of 'inappropriate' access – framed as medical interventions that young people may regret. This fails to recognise that firstly, prepubescent children and adolescents never access hormone replacement therapy. Secondly, hormone blockers (which will be explored fully later in this chapter) have the great advantage of being physically reversible (Hembree 2011), giving adolescents the time to establish their identity and needs without requiring certainty, and without eliminating the option of choosing to go through puberty associated with their assignment at birth. Hormone blockers do not need to be restricted to only the 'most certain' people – which also would risk only providing medical care to those patients who fulfil the most stereotypical trans narratives. Thirdly, trans or gender nonconforming identification frequently occurs without a person experiencing dysphoria that they feel would be helped by hormones and/or surgery, instead benefitting from a social transition only. Others still may not conceive their gender difference in terms of distress, but rather feel positive about articulating their gender, without being especially distressed by birth assignment. The medical services that exist are designed to provide a space where feelings about what works best for the individual can be explored, not to presume that everyone who identifies differently to their birth assignment needs the same pathway.

Different views exist on what constitutes being trans, even within the trans population. Some trans people claim that one is only trans if experiencing the need for a medical transition, because of gender dysphoria. These individuals and communities are sometimes known as **transmedicalists**, or **truscum** (Schmitt 2013). Such views fail to recognise that whilst medical interventions alleviate distress, trans identification does not *depend* on such distress (and therefore does not always involve medical transition).

Conversion therapy

Parents may fear for the wellbeing of their gender-diverse child for multiple reasons – concerns of bullying, anxiety that their child is making a mistake, or that being trans will make them vulnerable to discrimination throughout their life, or other concerns for their child's future. This may cause some parents to be tempted to seek out 'professionals' who will attempt to 'talk their child out' of gender non-conforming behaviour or a gender-diverse identity. This can also be practiced in more subtle ways – for example, the implicit scepticism that is recognisable to a young person if asked 'are you sure' for many months, sends a strong message that their gender expression or identity is undesirable. Any kind of therapy or attempt to 'cure' a young person of gender diverse behaviour or identification is 'conversion therapy' (also called 'reparative therapy'). This is definitely recognised as harmful to the wellbeing and development of young people. The 7th edition of the WPATH Standards of Care specifies that 'treatment aimed at trying to change a person's gender identity and expression to become more congruent with sex assigned at birth has been attempted in the past without success, particularly in the long term. Such treatment is now considered unethical' (Coleman *et al.* 2012, p.175). All professional bodies in the UK that govern the professional conduct of psychotherapeutic practice have signed a Memorandum of Understanding (MoU) which condemns conversion therapy in relation to sexuality and gender identity (British Psychoanalytic Council 2017, NHS England *et al.* 2015).

The importance of support

Higher life satisfaction, and a lower sense of being 'burdened' with a trans identity (in addition to fewer symptoms of depression) are associated with parental support of trans children and adolescents (Simons *et al.* 2013). It is a misconception to assume that 'support' constitutes immediate and un-nuanced delivery of hormones or surgeries to children or adolescents – this, quite simply, never occurs. As discussed in previous chapters, while hormones and/or surgeries can be essential for many trans people, they are not always needed or desired – yet this does not make a person 'less trans', if their gender identity still differs from their assignment at birth. When a child or adolescent shows differences in behaviour that are commonly associated with gender, it is important for families not to stigmatise this, or create an environment that positions such behaviour as 'strange' or 'not normal'. This goes beyond absence of punishment or admonishment, but must include recognition that reluctance, uneasiness, or scepticism expressed directly to a young person can have a significant impact on their sense of self-worth.

Children and adolescents are perceptive. Even in a family circumstance which does not prohibit say, toy choices, or cross-gender (associated) clothing, attempts to nudge a child in more normative directions will risk sending the message that there *are* 'right and wrong choices', and experience a sense of pressure from the family to 'be more normal'. This is also a problem when families feel that 'waiting until you're older' to allow greater gendered autonomy is a compromise. The only way to avoid risking a child's mental well-being is to embrace the child's identification and self-expression *in the moment*. It is entirely possible for a child's self-expression, the name or pronouns they use, or how they navigate the gendered world to change over time. This does not mean that enthusiastic support is not vital, and parents should be prepared to accept that any given gendered circumstance (non-binary; binary-oriented; not wanting medical interventions; being desperate for them) may be a step along the journey, or the consistent, persistent, insistent experience of their child.

That gender may evolve in a young person does not mean that all possibilities are equally likely. For example, strong accounts of embodied gender dysphoria do not simply disappear overnight. Additionally, if a young person has explicitly claimed a cross-gender (i.e. an AMAB child saying they are a girl, or vice versa), or trans identity, this will not simply 'go away on its own'. What is significantly more possible however, are shifts around the desire (or lack thereof) for medical intervention, and/or self-conception in binary, or non-binary terms. For example, a young AFAB person may initially identify as non-binary, and later come to identify as a (binary) trans boy. These shifts are likely to be slow, but may move in either direction (i.e. a trans boy or girl coming to later identify as a non-binary person).

Risks of an unsupportive environment

Without adequate support, young trans people can be extremely vulnerable. Repeated studies have shown rates of attempted suicide in trans people (young people and adults) between 25 and 48 per cent (Clements-Nolle *et al.* 2006, Grant *et al.* 2011, Grossman and D'Augelli 2007, Haas *et al.* 2014). The number of trans people who have considered ending their lives has been reported as 84 per cent (McNeil *et al.* 2012), and the numbers engaging in self-harm as 23 per cent (Di Ceglie *et al.* 2002). As mentioned in Chapter 5, recent evidence shows that children and adolescents who are supported in their gender identities experience depression at levels similar to the general population, and only incidentally higher levels of anxiety – which it is rational to ascribe to fear of potential stigma or discrimination, even when having a supportive family and peers (Olson *et al.* 2016).

Guidance for parents

In her book *The Gender Creative Child*, developmental and clinical psychologist and associate professor of paediatrics Dr. Diane Ehrensaft gives this advice:

> Basic ground rule for raising children: If we recognize the child we have, rather than the one we wished we had, and if we help our children build resilience to face the challenges before them, we put them in good stead to live a healthy and productive life. Now let's apply that ground rule to children's gender and their parents' role in gender health. [...] If you support your child's gender creativity, your children will do better, both psychologically and physically; if you fail to support their gender creativity, they will not do so well, both psychologically and physically.

> (Ehrensaft 2016, p.119)

Comprehensive guidance on how to best articulate support is unfortunately beyond the scope of this book, particularly given the vastly different challenges that different articulations of gender diversity may bring. Support can be accessed from a range of different organisations; however, **Mermaids** is the largest British organisation offering specific support to trans and gender-diverse children and adolescents and their families, and is run by parents of trans children. Their website – www.mermaidsuk.org.uk – includes tailored guidance for teenagers, parents, teachers, GPs, and social workers. The organisation **Gendered Intelligence** also specialises in support for trans people under the age of 21[2], with youth groups in London, Leeds, Bristol, and Hertfordshire. They also provide trans inclusion training, and guidance for schools, sixth forms, and further and higher education institutions. More information can be found on their website: genderedintelligence.co.uk.

Guidance for schools

Support from both the administration and peers are important for trans and gender diverse youth to thrive in the school environment. Brill and Pepper explain that:

> A welcoming and supportive school where bullying and teasing is not permitted and children are actively taught to respect and celebrate difference is the ideal environment for all children. This is especially true for gender-variant and transgender children, who frequently are the targets of teasing and bullying. A child cannot feel emotionally safe, and will most likely experience problems in learning, if they regularly experience discrimination at school.

> (Brill and Pepper 2008, p.153–4)

It has been shown that schools which foster a community organisation for the support of LGBTQ students (sometimes called 'gay-straight alliances', although this erases the inclusion of trans and bisexual youth) results in better experiences of school and lower psychological distress (Heck *et al.* 2011). Supportive educators, LGBT-inclusive curricula (particularly sex and

---

2   There is also an 18–30 group specifically in London.

relationship education) and comprehensive, lesbian, gay, bisexual, and trans-specific anti-bullying and anti-harassment policies can also significantly improve the experiences of trans students at school (Greytak *et al.* 2013).

In keeping with the Equality Act, schools should allow trans young people access to gender-segregated spaces (such as bathrooms) which match the identity of the young person. Failure to validate a trans young person by not considering trans girls as girls, or trans boys as boys, poses serious risks to that young person's wellbeing, as discussed earlier in this chapter. Young people with non-binary identities should have access to gender-neutral facilities, and/or be able to use the space they feel is most appropriate for them. Unless a young trans person requests it, asking or requiring trans young people to only use wheelchair-accessible bathrooms or staff bathrooms is inappropriate. Further, schools with uniforms should allow a trans young person to wear the gendered uniform which matches their gender identity.

Specific guidance on The Equality Act 2010 and schools has been written by the Department for Education, and can be downloaded via this link: www.mermaidsuk.org.uk/assets/media/Equality_Act_Advice_Schools.pdf – this document makes it clear that it is 'unlawful for schools to treat pupils less favourably because of their gender reassignment and that schools will have to factor in gender reassignment when considering their obligations under the Equality Duty' (p. 17). A 'Trans Inclusion Schools Toolkit' has also been created with Brighton and Hove City Council, which can be downloaded (and used beyond the context of Brighton and Hove) here: www.mermaidsuk.org.uk/assets/media/Trans-Inclusion-Schools-Toolkit.pdf

Further Transgender Guidance for Schools is also available from the Intercom Trust, most recently revised July 2015 – www.intercomtrust.org.uk/item/55. This includes guidance beyond the scope of this book, including absence from school or college, sports and physical education, dealing with the concerns of staff, families and carers, transition in the context of a single-sex school, school trips, etc.

Guidance for clinicians – referrals

While adults and older adolescents ask for GIC referral themselves and often have a long-established disidentification with their assignment at birth (even if they're not entirely certain whether they may identify in binary or non-binary terms, or if/what gender-affirming medical interventions would be right for them), childhood and young adolescent referrals are typically sought by the child's parent(s) or guardian(s), or sometimes by a CAMHS clinician, or the young person's school. Referrals can be accepted from anyone apart from the parent or young person themselves – including any health professional, and the organisation Mermaids.

England: The Gender Identity Development Service (GIDS)

London address: The Tavistock Centre, 120 Belsize Lane, London, NW3 5BA

Leeds address: 8 Park Square, Leeds, LS1 2LH

Telephone: 020 8938 2030/1 (London), 0113 247 1955 (Leeds)

Email: gids@tavi-port.nhs.uk (for both locations)

Website: gids.nhs.uk

Provided by: The Tavistock and Portman NHS Foundation Trust

Average waiting time for first appointment (October 2017): at least 12 months

Accessibility: For families with a low income, the clinic can pay for train travel if qualifying criteria are met. Full information may be found at: gids.nhs.uk/how-claim-travel-expenses

The Gender Identity Development Service has two main sites, based in London and Leeds. A satellite clinic is also run in Exeter, with a possibility of other local arrangements such as Cardiff, Bristol, or Birmingham (subject to space and staff availability) for patients who live far away from the main sites.

The GIDS has a referral form, which can be downloaded by clicking the indicated link at the bottom of this page: gids.nhs.uk/referrals

The national contract which the GIDS has covers referrals from England, Scotland, and Northern Ireland, which means that no local funding approval is needed. However, funding confirmation does need to be established prior to an appointment for people living in Wales (or other territories, or countries). The funding application usually needs to be done by the referring clinician.

Scotland: The Sandyford Clinic

6 Sandyford Place, Sauchiehall Street, Glasgow, G3 7NB

Telephone: for self-referrals – 0141 211 8137, for general enquiries – 0141 211 8130, for professional referral on a patient's behalf – 0141 211 8646

Email: sandyford@ggc.scot.nhs.uk

Website: www.sandyford.org/sandyford-sexual-health-services/what-are-our-services/gender-identity-service

Provided by: NHS Greater Glasgow and Clyde

Average waiting time for first appointment (June 2017): not available

Accessibility: NHS Greater Glasgow and Clyde has made web resources about the service more accessible, see: www.sandyford.org/accessibility

Sandyford GIC allows for self-referrals (including parents on behalf of their child) to be made – it is not necessary for a GP or other health practitioner to make the referral for a patient. An initial appointment can be arranged by telephone.

Northern Ireland: KOI – Knowing Our Identity, Gender Identity Development Service for Northern Ireland

Knowing Our Identity, Beechroft, Foster Green Site, 110 Saintfield Road, Belfast, BT8 6HD

Telephone: 02890 638000

Email: BrackenburnClinic@belfasttrust.hscni.net

Website: www.belfasttrust.hscni.net/services/GenderIdentity. htm

Provided by: Belfast Health and Social Care Trust

Average waiting time for first appointment (April 2015): 7 weeks

Accessibility: no specific information available

The standard referral pathway is for a GP to make a referral to Child and Adolescent Mental Health Services (CAMHS). CAMHS then make a referral to KOI. However, young people and their families can contact the services directly to discuss the possibilities of accessing referral. KOI offer counselling, other mental health services, and support for families and peers. Hormones can potentially be accessed for young people who are 15 or older, following assessment.

More information can be accessed from the charity **GenderJam NI**, run by and for young trans people in Northern Ireland. They can be contacted via their website: genderjam.org.uk

The Tanner stages

These scales function to approximately measure progression through puberty via the measurement of primary and secondary sexual characteristics. Three scales are used – development of external genitalia in young people assigned male at birth, breast development in young people assigned female at birth, and pubic hair growth in both. The scales are not age dependent, and are important for the clinically appropriate timing of hormone blockers in children and adolescents. Each of the scales is divided into five stages, with stage 1 indicating pre-pubertal anatomy, and stage 5 indicating full adult development.

Table 6.1: Penis and testes development for AMAB young people

Tanner Stage 1	Pre-pubertal; testes smaller than 2.5 cm on long axis, no penis growth
Tanner Stage 2	Earliest scrotal enlargement (2.5 to 3.2 cm); scrotal skin reddens and becomes thinner
Tanner Stage 3	Penal growth (~6 cm); further testicular growth (~3.6 cm)
Tanner Stage 4	Continued penal (~10 cm) and testicular growth (4.1–4.5 cm)
Tanner Stage 5	Mature genital (~15 cm) and gonadal (~4.5 cm or more) sizes – note there can be great variation in genital size with no pathology.

Table 6.2: Breast development for AFAB young people

Tanner Stage 1	Pre-pubertal; absence of glandular tissue
Tanner Stage 2	Formation of the breast bud (thelarche); areola begins widening
Tanner Stage 3	Elevation of breast and extension beyond areola, continued areolar widening
Tanner Stage 4	Continued increase in breast size and elevation, secondary mound forms under areola (nipple development)
Tanner Stage 5	Adult breast size reached; areola returns to contour concurrent with surrounding breast tissue with a projecting central nipple (papilla).

Table 6.3: Pubic hair growth for all young people

Tanner Stage 1	None
Tanner Stage 2	Long downy hair
Tanner Stage 3	Increased in amount, pigmentation, and curling
Tanner Stage 4	Adult in type but not in distribution
Tanner Stage 5	Adult in type, extending to the medial surface of thighs

Tanner stages provide guidance for the appropriate timing of when blockers and/or HRT may be safely prescribed for trans young people. Tanner stages are preferable as a system of deciding when to begin blockers, due to differences in the timing of puberty when based on age. An age limit risks forcing a young person who is experiencing distressing and irreversible aspects of pubertal change below a particular age limit to wait until being old enough, by which time some Tanner stages may already have been moved through. Tanner stage 2 should be reached prior to the initiation of blockers. Any time after this level of development has been reached can be an appropriate time to prescribe, based on the needs of the individual patient. Because of their reversible nature, prescription of hormone blockers can also be appropriate as part of a diagnostic process (thus certainty of a desire to transition is not a requirement for blockers), to allow a young person more time to establish whether HRT is desirable for them (Delemarre-van de Waal and Cohen-Kettenis 2006).

Puberty/hormone blockers

This group of medications was originally used exclusively in the management of precocious puberty.[3] Blockers can be used with transgender children or adolescents to prevent the onset of a puberty which would be undesirable and cause physical dysphoria. Due to their reversible nature, blockers are also an appropriate prescription for young people who are negotiating their gender identity, and can benefit from time to reflect (and continue to mentally grow and mature) on their needs, without puberty causing potentially unwanted development. Use of blockers can significantly reduce the need for particular medical interventions used in adulthood as part of medical transition – such as electrolysis, laser hair removal or facial feminisation surgeries for transfeminine people, or mastectomy for transmasculine people. It has been noted that 'suppression causes no irreversible or harmful changes in physical development and puberty resumes readily if hormonal suppression is stopped' (Hembree 2011, p.725). Fertility will also return when hormone blockers are stopped (Butler 2017). Blockers will not reverse any pubertal processes that have already happened, but simply pause them. Some (currently anecdotal) evidence from young people who have received hormone blockers may suggest that AFAB young people may experience a

---

3 Precocious puberty is defined as the onset of puberty for AMAB children before age 9, and AFAB children before age 8. This can be caused in multiple pathological ways, or be simple variation, yet still possibly undesirable or distressing for the child.

reduction in breast tissue, while some AMAB young people have reported thinning of body and facial hair.

General side effects

Some (small) decrease in bone density is a possible side effect of hormone blockers. This is due to sex hormones playing a role in the uptake of calcium as part of bone growth during puberty. This reduction will recover when the blocker is stopped or if hormones are administered as part of a medical transition. Dual energy x-ray absorptiometry (DEXA) scanning can be used to check bone mineral density. In the context of University College London Hospital (UCLH – via GIDS), a scan of the spine is required before starting the blocker, which is repeated annually for as long as the blocker is maintained. Recent research suggests that the impact of blockers on bone strength is minimal.

The impact of hormone blockers on height is non-intuitive. If blockers are started after a person has had their growth spurt (associated with Tanner Stage 2 or 3 in people assigned female at birth, and Tanner stage 3 or 4 in people assigned male at birth) then impact on height will be minimal. If blockers are started before this, then rather than stopping growth, the period of time with increased growth is stretched out, such that a taller adult height is likely to be attained. This may be desirable (for example, in binary-oriented AFAB transmasculine people), unwanted, or a point of ambivalence.

Consent to treatment – Gillick competence

Any patient who is 16 or older is legally entitled to consent to (or refuse) their own treatment. The only exception to where consent can be overruled is where refusal of treatment is deemed to lead to death or severe permanent injury, in keeping with the Mental Capacity Act (2005). However, people under the age of 16 can consent to their own treatment, provided they are capable of understanding what is involved in the treatment. Young people deemed capable of understanding what a medical treatment will do to their bodies are said to be 'Gillick competent', which was established in 1985 via a legally binding court case (for England and Wales) taken to the House of Lords. This established that contraception could be prescribed to under 16s at the doctor's discretion, without parental knowledge or consent. The Age of Legal Capacity (Scotland) Act 1991 provides a similar model for Scotland. Northern Ireland also follows the model of Gillick competence.[4]

With regards to ethical medical practice and the prescription of *hormones* (rather than hormone blockers) for under 16s, the case can be made that if the patient is Gillick competent, and has reached Tanner stage 2, and fulfils the criteria for gender dysphoria in adults and adolescents, the most reasonable conclusion is to provide treatment, given lack of contraindications. The prescription of hormones, if relevant, on a case-by-case basis to under 16s is common in Canada, although practitioners do experience structural barriers to providing care for their trans patients (Snelgrove *et al.* 2012). The potential prescription of hormones in under 16s is a controversial topic, however the necessity of fulfilling the above criteria, which includes the necessity of persistent, insistent, consistent experience of gender dysphoria, makes this a low-risk decision, particularly because a minimum of several months of treatment are required before any pubertal development will be seen. The most extensive and irreversible of changes occur over a timeframe of years, such that in the highly unlikely circumstance of desistance (following such a firm fulfilment of clinical need) the patient can simply stop treatment. The harm that results from the withholding of treatment is considerably greater than the risk of inappropriate treatment when following WPATH guidelines, but with flexibility around numerical age rather than physical and mental maturity. For the trans adolescent who knows their needs beyond reasonable doubt, being able to enter the desired puberty at an age concordant with the onset of puberty of their cisgender peers likely offers further mental and societal benefits, rather than the arbitrary prevention of pubertal development until the 16th birthday is reached (and often in practice, considerably later than this).

---

4   See www.medicalprotection.org/uk/resources/factsheets/northern-ireland/ northern-ireland-factsheets/uk-ni-consent-children-and-young-people   for more information on consent under 18 in Northern Ireland.

Criteria for prescription

The 7th edition of the WPATH Standards of Care provides these minimum criteria in the prescription of puberty-suppressing hormones:

1. the adolescent has demonstrated a long-lasting and intense pattern of gender nonconformity or gender dysphoria (whether suppressed or expressed)

2. gender dysphoria emerged or worsened with the onset of puberty

3. any coexisting psychological, medical, or social problems that could interfere with treatment (e.g., that may compromise treatment adherence) have been addressed, such that the adolescent's situation and functioning are stable enough to start treatment

4. the adolescent has given informed consent and, particularly when the adolescent has not reached the age of medical consent, the parents or other caretakers or guardians have consented to the treatment and are involved in supporting the adolescent through the treatment process.

Fertility

Young people and their parents may often be concerned about the ramifications that blockers, hormones, and transition generally may have for fertility. GIDS clinicians recommend that families ask their GP for a referral to fertility counselling. This specific service can provide more information about fertility preservation options. However, most clinical commissioning groups (CCGs – regional bodies who plan and commission local healthcare services) do not fund fertility counselling for trans youth (yet do for other young people with conditions requiring treatment that can impact fertility, such as cancer).

UCLH currently have the capacity to store sperm, but not eggs. This discrepancy in equality of service is due to the UCLH fertility department not having the provisions to store eggs at all – the department was not originally for this purpose, but a pathway was created for sperm storage to make the best of resources that were already present.

Should a fertility clinic be accessed (via the NHS or privately), there are specific provisions that staff may consider to make their services more appropriate and accessible. Examples include the possibility of trans youth focussed time slots to avoid discomfort (e.g. a young AMAB trans person in a busy waiting room with many adult men), or removing any pornographic material from a room that a young person may be asked to use.

Role of the GP in managing blockers and hormones for young people

It is requested the GPs prescribe and administer blockers and/or hormones in transgender young people at the instruction of the GIDS (or other regionally-specific specialist services). Unlike the adult context, the UCLH (in conjunction with the GIDS) will monitor the blood work, bones, and side effects experienced by young people in England. GPs do not need to perform monitoring for patients who are under 18.

Gonadotropin-releasing hormone (GnRH) analogues

Specifically, all of the GnRH analogues used for pubertal suppression are GnRH antagonists. These bind to the GnRH receptor, downregulating hormones called gonadotropins, which then serves to inhibit the hypothalamic-pituitary-gonadal (HPG) axis[5], decreasing production of androgens, estrogens, and progestogens. This family of drugs are the preferred method of puberty suppression in adolescents (Hembree *et al.* 2009). They are suitable for prescription in young people who were AMAB or AFAB. GnRH analogues may also be prescribed in trans adults to block endogenous hormone production, in conjunction with estrogen or testosterone HRT.

All medications carry a risk of allergic reaction, but this is rare (severe rash, itching, swelling, difficulty breathing).

For readers without a medical or scientific background, it is helpful to know that substances prepared and sold as medications

---

5   A system of three glands which work together to control hormone production.

often have multiple different names for the same thing. There is the **scientific name** (such as estradiol valerate), which is the name of the specific molecule. This will be the active ingredient (or one of several) in a preparation, the pill, patch, injection etc. sold by a company. These preparations have **brand names** which vary between different companies, and also different countries. Preparations may have different names to indicate the active ingredient is at a different dose, or combined with other molecules (for example, estradiol is often combined with another molecule called a progestin, of which there are many different types). In the subtitles below, the first name given is the scientific name, with major brand names given in brackets, or otherwise indicated with a 'registered' symbol – ®.

Triptorelin (Decapeptyl® SR, Gonapeptyl® depot)[6]

These are the only blocker preparations which UCLH currently use with the young people under their care. Triptorelin is also sold under the name **Trelstar®**. Gonapeptyl® depot comes in 3.75mg doses, and can be administered preferably via subcutaneous injection, with intra-muscular injection also possible. The dose should be administered every three to four weeks. Decapeptyl® SR comes in 11.25 mg doses, and is delivered by deep intra-muscular injection every 10 to 12 weeks.

Potential side effects

For decapeptyl® and gonapeptyl®, very common (more than 1 in 10 patients) side effects include:

- hot flushes/sweating
- difficulty sleeping
- headaches
- tiredness.

For decapeptyl® and gonapeptyl®, common (between 1 and 10 of 100 patients) sides effects include:

---

6 'Depot' indicates a slow-release injection.

- nausea

- pain (lower abdomen, joints, and/or bones)

- mood changes

- skin reactions at the injection site.

Side effects vary in commonality based on assignment at birth, and the time in puberty when blockers are begun – young people starting a blocker later (more advanced through the Tanner stages) are more likely to experience side effects. For more detailed information please see the manufacturer information[7], which does give some differences between decapeptyl® and gonapeptyl®.

Contraindications

- Known hypersensitivity to triptorelin or excipients

- undiagnosed vaginal bleeding

- known or suspected pregnancy.

Goserelin (Zoladex®)

Pre-filled syringe applicators containing Goserelin Acetate (as an implant) are available in two doses – 3.6 mg and 10.8 mg. A trained health professional injects the implant into the thigh, subcutaneously. The implant lasts for 12 weeks.

Potential side effects

Note that the patient information leaflet for Zoladex® states it should 'not be given to children'. This is because the use of Zoladex® to delay the onset of puberty in gender-dysphoric adolescents is currently an off-label prescription. This is legal, and a common medical practice. Information given here on side-effects

---

7   Manufacturer information for decapeptyl® SR 11.25mg can be read at: https://www.medicines.org.uk/emc/PIL.13849.latest.pdf. Manufacturer information for gonapeptyl® depot 3.75mg can be read at: https://www.medicines.org.uk/emc/PIL.17988.latest.pdf

is not exhaustive, and has been interpreted for greatest relevance to adolescents – for example, risks connected to heavy drinking, smoking, or sexual function are not discussed.

Very common (more than 1 in 10 people) side effects are:

- hot flushes/sweating

- skin reactions at the injection site.

Common (up to 1 in 10 people) side effects include:

- tingling in fingers and toes

- headaches

- rashes

- joint pain

- mood changes

- Blood pressure changes.

Side effects vary in commonality based on assignment at birth. For exhaustive information please see the full manufacturer information.[8]

Contraindications

- Known hypersensitivity to goserelin or excipients (substances included in the injection's preparation)

- undiagnosed vaginal bleeding

- known or suspected pregnancy.

Leuprorelin (Prostap® SR DCS) [9]

Prostap® SR DCS is delivered as an injection, and can be either subcutaneous or intra-muscular. Available doses are 3.75mg or

---

8   The package leaflet for Zoladex® 3.6 mg implant can be read at: https://www.medicines.org.uk/emc/PIL.10755.latest.pdf

9   SR stands for 'slow release' and indicates the activity of the drug occurs over a longer period of time, through suspension in a carrier liquid. DCS stands for Dual-Chamber pre-filled Syringe.

11.25mg. The lower dose should be administered every three to four weeks whilst the higher dose every 10 to 12 weeks.

Potential side effects

If a patient is diabetic, Prostap® can aggravate the condition, requiring more frequent blood glucose monitoring.

Very common (more than 1 in 10 people) side effects are:

- hot flushes/sweating

- weight changes

- tiredness

- skin reactions at the injection site.

Common (up to 1 in 10 people) side effects include:

- nausea

- headaches

- joint pain

- loss of appetite

- difficulty sleeping.

Side effects vary in commonality based on assignment at birth. For exhaustive information please see the full manufacturer information.[10]

Contraindications

- Known hypersensitivity to leuprorelin or excipients

- undiagnosed vaginal bleeding

- known or suspected pregnancy.

---

10 The package leaflet for Prostap® 3 DCS can be read at: https://www.medicines. org.uk/emc/PIL.24677.latest.pdf

Progestins

Progestins are synthetic hormones which can bind to the progesterone receptor. This inhibits the gonadotropins, resulting in the inhibition of androgens, estrogens, and progestogens as with the GnRH antagonists. This class of hormones has a history of use as contraception, and to prevent endometrial hyperplasia in menopausal-related HRT for cis women.

Medroxyprogesterone Acetate (MPA) (Provera®, Depo-Provera®)

The 7th edition of the WPATH Standards of Care specifically named MPA as a suitable alternative pubertal suppression (Coleman *et al.* 2012, p.177). MPA can be delivered by intramuscular injection. Depo-Provera® can be sourced at 150mg/ml for injection every 12 weeks.

Oral preparations of MPA also exist, however this use has been primarily as oral contraception and may be in combination with conjugated estrogens (such as **Indivina®** or **Tridestra®**), which are undesirable for the cessation of puberty in the adolescent. Combinations of MPA and estradiol may be appropriate for adult AMAB transitions, as these preparations stop testosterone production whilst providing estradiol. For adults, an oral dose of 5 to 10 mg daily has been recommended (Kreukels *et al.* 2014).

Potential side effects

Very common (more than 1 in 10 people) side effects are:

- nervousness

- weight changes

- headache

- stomach ache.

Common (up to 1 in 10 people) side effects include:

- nausea

- dizziness

- depression

- weakness

- acne.

For more detailed information please see the manufacturer information.[11]

Contraindications

- Known hypersensitivity to MPA or excipients

- undiagnosed vaginal bleeding

- known or suspected pregnancy

- hormone-dependent cancers

- liver disease.

Additional prescribed interventions

Contraceptive pill (varied types)

Many young AFAB trans people are particularly concerned with stopping their period due to its exacerbation of gender dysphoria. There are multiple types of oral contraception which are potentially appropriate for this purpose.

Eflornithine (Vaniqa®)

Vaniqa® cream is a topical treatment for facial hirsutism in women, but is also an appropriate prescription for young AMAB trans people who are experiencing distress from the development of facial hair.

---

11 Manufacturer information for Depo-Provera® 150mg/ml can be read at: https://www.medicines.org.uk/emc/PIL.11127.latest.pdf

Chapter 7

Gender Affirmation

Hormone Replacement Therapy, and Non-Surgical Interventions

This chapter goes into detail on all non-surgical interventions which adult trans people may need to access. The most common of these, which the vast majority of medically-transitioning trans people need to access, are estrogen or testosterone prescription. While primary care practitioners are responsible for the prescription of hormones and the monitoring of bloodwork, other forms of non-surgical interventions are more a question of information provision and signposting. This includes information about hair removal, voice therapy, chest binding for AFAB trans people, and the use of prostheses in alleviating dysphoria.

Criteria for hormone prescription

The Interim Gender Dysphoria Protocol and Service Guidelines 2013/14 states these criteria for hormone prescription:

1. persistent, well-documented gender dysphoria

2. capacity to make a fully informed decision and to consent for treatment

3. aged at least 17 years[1]

---

1 Note that these criteria are exclusively in the context of adult services. The service protocol for the Tavistock and Portman young person's service (as of early 2018) states that young people may have access to hormones 'around 16', allowing them to be put forward for hormones at around 15 years and 10 months. This changed from 'after 16' in the previous protocol.

4. if significant medical or mental health concerns are present, they must be reasonably well controlled. (NHS England 2013, p.16)

Patients also need to be registered with a GP. These criteria match those advised in the 7th edition of the WPATH Standards of Care (Coleman *et al.* 2012, p.187). As discussed in the previous chapter, it is problematic for an arbitrary age restriction to be placed on hormone access rather than assessment of the evidence in each individual case for benefit versus risk, where Gillick competence and Tanner stage 2 are met, in addition to the additional diagnostic criteria. At the time of writing, consultation on a new set of Service Guidelines had begun. Clinicians should double-check the most up-to-date protocol as the age limit may drop, or be replaced with other factors.

The GP's role in hormone provision

Prescription of hormones is done by a GP, rather than by GIC practitioners (who are not commissioned to do so). There are no National Institute for Health and Care Excellence (NICE) guidelines for gender dysphoria, however the information presented here is cross-referenced with current UK Gender Dysphoria Protocols, the WPATH Standards of Care, the Best Practice Guidelines from the Royal College of Psychiatrists, and Clinical Practice Guidelines from the Endocrine Society in particular.[2]

Guidance on referring a patient to a GIC is given in Chapter 4. Following this, the GIC will contact the GP to advise hormone prescription if desired by the patient and deemed appropriate. There are a range of different circumstances where a patient presents to a GP requesting hormones, and it can be entirely appropriate and medically necessary for the GP to provide a prescription for an unlimited period, and provide blood testing to ensure correct hormone levels, **without** referral to a GIC, or in combination with a referral, but prior to an appointment being given or attended. These circumstances are explained in turn.

---

2   The General Medical Council have published new guidance for primary care practitioners on prescribing which can be found here: https://www.gmc-uk. org/ethical-guidance/ethical-hub/trans-healthcare#prescribing (see the other tabs for other useful information on aspects of transgender healthcare).

When a patient has already been referred to and seen by a GIC

Following assessment by a GIC, a specialist will write to the patient's GP to formally state that a diagnosis of 'Transsexualism'[3] has been made, and that the GP should make an appropriate (indefinite) hormone prescription for the patient, and perform regular blood monitoring to ensure that sex hormones are in the normal ranges for the gender with which the patient identifies. Some GPs may feel they lack the experience to prescribe hormones to trans people – it is for these practitioners in particular that this book hopes to support in gaining the confidence to help their trans patients. The GP can be in contact with the patient's GIC for guidance if necessary. Some non-binary patients will still desire cross-sex HRT at the same dosages as binary-oriented trans people. More detail on non-binary hormone dosing can be found later in this chapter.

When a trans person has changed GP practice and has a history of hormone therapy

For trans people who need access to hormones, they are a lifelong treatment regimen. Therefore, there are many trans people who have been discharged from GICs due to having completed the medical transition process they require. These are people who have been through a process of referral and diagnosis – in some cases, many decades ago – and accessed hormones routinely since then. **If a patient's records show they have previously been prescribed hormones by another GP at their previous practice, GPs should continue this routine without diagnostic (re)assessment**. The practitioner may deem it appropriate to take their own history/a brief review, or arrange blood tests in order to establish the most up-to-date records in the new practice. The Good Practice Guidelines for the Assessment and Treatment of Adults with Gender Dysphoria (Royal College of Psychiatrists 2014) specifically

---

3   This dated terminology is used because adult GICs in the UK currently use the ICD-10 (published in 1990) rather than the DSM-5 (published in 2013, which uses the diagnostic term Gender Dysphoria). The ICD-11 (due for publication in or before 2019) will replace transsexualism with the term 'gender incongruence'.

states 'When patients move between clinical services, appropriate endocrine treatment should continue to be offered' (p.28).

When a bridging prescription is necessary

The UK Good Practice Guidelines for the Assessment and Treatment of Adults with Gender Dysphoria (Royal College of Psychiatrists 2014) specifies that 'the GP or other medical practitioner involved in the patient's care may prescribe 'bridging' endocrine treatments as part of a holding and harm reduction strategy while the patient awaits specialised endocrinology or other gender identity treatment and/or confirmation of hormone prescription elsewhere or from patient records' (p. 25).

'Bridging prescription' is a phrase generally not used by GIC clinicians to mean 'starting estrogens or testosterone'. At Charing Cross, it's used to mean a group of medical treatments broadly similar to those used in child/adolescent services: anti-androgens such as finasteride, menses-suppressing preparations such as norethisterone, less commonly GnRH analogues. In the wider trans community, though, it's often assumed to mean 'the same hormones, in the same doses, that are prescribed at a GIC'.

It is justifiable for a practitioner to interpret a bridging prescription as being a prescription for estrogen or testosterone. This may be regarded as a form of harm reduction where patients may otherwise be likely to, or already be, self-medicating with hormones without monitoring. In line with harm reduction policy, it is strongly recommended that a GP who has been asked for a bridging prescription check for contraindications (see later in this chapter, under estrogen or testosterone as appropriate). If contraindications are found, the patient should be made aware, such that they understand the associated risks with HRT for them. GPs should appreciate the risks associated with not prescribing hormones, including in cases of absolute or relative contraindications. Prescription may still be appropriate where the benefits of HRT outweigh the risks.

If no contraindications are found, GPs should then check that the patient is informed regarding the changes that can be expected with long-term hormone prescription, and that the patient understands that some of these changes are irreversible.

This is to ensure that informed consent is obtained. The UK Good Practice Guidelines for the Assessment and Treatment of Adults with Gender Dysphoria (Royal College of Psychiatrists 2014) states that 'patients are presumed, unless proven otherwise, capable of consenting to treatment' (p.14). When informed consent is obtained, the GP should prescribe the patient the appropriate hormone, and arrange for regular blood work to ensure appropriate hormone levels.

An important dimension is that ultimately, the doctor signing the prescription has to *understand* the therapy – specifically, the risks of prescribing versus the risks of not prescribing – and agree/believe that the latter outweighs the former. This is often a straightforward process, but may not always be – which is reflected in those trans people who ask for referral to a GIC but are very uncertain about what interventions (if any) they want/need. This may also change over time.

When a patient is self-medicating

Waiting times for all GICs in Britain are notoriously long, frequently years for a first appointment. Untreated gender dysphoria can cause extreme distress, risking mental health and dramatically increasing the risks of self-harm and suicidality (Ellis *et al.* 2015, McNeil *et al.* 2012). This is particularly the case for trans people who are highly certain of their need for medical transition. When faced with these circumstances, some trans people purchase hormones from the internet. This carries the risks of taking hormones with no assessment for contraindications, no blood work to establish an appropriate individual dosage regimen, and no regulation of the source of the hormones. It has also been shown that patients who self-medicate with estrogen are significantly more likely to later request mammoplasty, which is likely related to sub-optimal breast growth related to poor dosage management (Seal *et al.* 2012). From the trans person's perspective, these risks may pale into insignificance compared to the experience of gender dysphoria. Self-medication is often something of a 'last resort', when a trans person has already reached a breaking-point. GPs should work to consider these circumstances from their patient's perspective. Many trans people are familiar with the risks that self-medication may pose (rather than having acted 'irresponsibly') yet the experience of dysphoria puts them in the literal position of 'access hormones or die'.

It is therefore prudent to consider HRT as a life-saving medication for many trans people. GPs should advise a trans person who is self-medicating of the risks of doing so, and establish whether the trans person has any contraindications for the hormones they are taking. In line with harm reduction, GPs should strongly consider providing a bridging prescription, and monitoring bloodwork for self-medicating patients.

Estrogen (Estradiol)

Estrogen is not a single compound. Rather, the estrogens are a family of molecules of different types, subdivided into steroidal and non-steroidal estrogens. Endogenous (produced by the body) estrogens are all steroidal. The three most important estrogens are estrone, estradiol, and estriol – also known as 'E1', 'E2', and 'E3', respectively. Hormone prescription for trans women or non-binary (AMAB) people uses only **estradiol**.

The goal of treatment (in terms of biochemistry) is to produce a blood serum estradiol concentration within the 'normal' range for cis women. This range is **350–750 pmol/L**.[4] Therefore, 'providers are encouraged to consult with their local lab(s) to obtain hormone level reference ranges for both "male" and "female" norms, and then apply the correct range when interpreting results based on the current hormonal sex, rather than the sex of registration' (Deutsch 2017, no pagination). Additionally, for many people, treatment with estradiol will suppress testosterone levels, without the need for an additional prescription of an antiandrogen. The desired testosterone level that should be maintained in trans women and non-binary (AMAB) people is less than 3 nmol/L. If testosterone levels do not drop adequately with estradiol prescription alone, then an antiandrogen prescription is also necessary – see later in this chapter.

---

4   Where an estradiol concentration is given in pg/ml, this can be converted to pmol/L by multiplying the pg/ml value by 3.676.

As with the discussions in Chapter 6, estradiol is the *scientific name* for the specific molecule, which may be the active ingredient in lots of different preparations with their own *brand names*. Brand names are indicated by a 'registered' symbol – ®.

Contraindications for Estradiol prescription

- Hemiplegic migraine
- stroke with aura
- breast cancer
- any estrogen-sensitive cancer
- a history of thrombosis
- a history of a blood-clotting disorder
- a history of heart attack, stroke, or angina
- a history of liver disease, where liver function tests still show abnormal levels
- porphyria
- obesity
- smoking
- known hypersensitivity to estradiol or excipients.

Baseline tests prior to Estradiol prescription

Blood pressure, full blood count, urea and electrolytes, liver function tests, fasting blood glucose or HbA1C (glycated haemoglobin), lipid profile, thyroid function, serum testosterone, estradiol, prolactin, LH, and FSH. For ongoing blood test monitoring, timing depends on the methods of estradiol delivery. Tests should be taken four hours after estrogen tablets are taken, or 48 hours after a new patch, or four to six hours after gel application, ensuring gel was not applied to the arms (Seal 2007). Blood tests are advised to be done every four months for the first year, six-monthly for the following three years, and annually after that (Greener 2014).

Table 7.1: Changes to be expected with Estradiol

Bodily change:	First changes seen:	Little change expected after:	Reversibility
Decreased spontaneous erections	1 to 3 months	3 to 6 months	Reverts if estrogen stopped
Decrease in sex drive[4] and changed experience of orgasm	1 to 3 months	1 to 2 years	Reverts if estrogen stopped
Male-pattern baldness slows and stops (minor or no regrowth)	1 to 3 months	1 to 2 years	Reverts if estrogen stopped
Loss of muscle mass and definition, and decreased strength	3 to 6 months	1 to 2 years	Reverts if estrogen stopped
Breast tissue development	3 to 6 months	2 to 3+ years	Permanent, would require surgery
Decrease in genital and gonad size	3 to 6 months	2 to 3 years	Reverts if estrogen stopped
Softer skin, less oil production	3 to 6 months	Unknown	Reverts if estrogen stopped
Redistribution of body fat	3 to 6 months	2 to 5 years	Reverts if estrogen stopped
Thinning and slower growth of facial and body hair	6 to 12 months	>3 years	Reverts if estrogen stopped
Decreased sperm production	Variable	Variable	Variable

It is noteworthy that pace and severity of changes may possibly escalate following any surgery where the testes are removed. The removal of endogenous testosterone production can mean transfeminine people can experience another 'wave' of

---

5   This will be different for a young person who has been on a blocker prior to taking estradiol. They will actually experience an increase in sex drive when they start taking estrogen, as the blocker will have cut sex drive completely.

development. The figures above may not be representative of the great deal of variation that is possible – accounts have been made of breast growth continuing five to seven years after beginning hormones, due to moderate growth post-genital surgery, and then slow growth for some years after that.

Different preparations, doses, and deliveries

Tablets

Different brands of the same formulation (estradiol valerate, or estradiol hemihydrate) are available, as 1 or 2 mg pills. A dose of 1 to 6 mg daily is recommended (Greener 2014). Dosage depends on initial circulating estradiol levels. Patches or topical gel may be preferable in patients over 40, smokers, or AMAB trans people with a history of liver disease, as those routes of delivery lower the risks of thrombosis or liver problems. These risks are why the preparation of estrogen called **premarin** (infamously manufactured from pregnant mares' urine) is no longer recommended.

Estradiol tablets can come as *estrogen-only* preparations, or as *combination* preparations. This is because all preparations of estradiol have been made with HRT for cisgender women in mind, in management of menopausal symptoms. The combination preparations each contain a type of **progestin** (a synthetic progestogen which behaves like the hormone progesterone). For cisgender women who have a womb, both of these hormones can be necessary. For cisgender women who have had a hysterectomy, estrogen-only HRT is possible. **Trans women and AMAB non-binary people must be prescribed an estradiol-only preparation**. This is because progestins pose an increased risk of thromboembolic incidents, and cardiovascular mortality (Manson *et al.* 2003). All patches and gel are estradiol only.

Appropriate estradiol-only preparations in tablet form include **Progynova®**, **Elleste®**, **Climaval®**, and **Zumenon®**.

Patches

A prescription between **50–200 micrograms (µg) twice per week** should be given, depending on initial blood test results. Because any dose over 100µg requires more than one patch, prescribers and pharmacy dispensers should be clear that this is still only one prescription (and therefore only one charge for patients who pay for their prescriptions) despite receiving two different doses. In cases where only some patch concentrations are available and others are not, it is possible to cut patches in half without impacting their effect (e.g. a 100 µg patch could be cut in half, and used with a complete 100 µg patch if someone has a prescription of 150 µg (Durand *et al.* 2012, Vancouver Hospital and Health Sciences Centre 2002)). **Whether it is possible to cut a patch in half without affecting its function depends on the type of patch.** In short, in the context of HRT, **matrix patches may be cut, but reservoir patches should never be cut**.[6] Patches should be changed twice per week (every 3 to 4 days). Patches should be applied to a dry area of the lower abdomen. When replacing the patch, use a different patch of skin to avoid irritation. Patches should never be applied to the upper body or arms.

There are multiple different available brands of estradiol in patch form. **Estradot®** transdermal patches come in concentrations of 25, 37.5, 50, 75, and 100 micrograms (µg). **Estraderm®**, and **Evorel®** transdermal patches come in concentrations of 25, 50, 75, and 100 µg. Availability may vary over time and between different pharmacies.

Topical gel

An example brand of estradiol as a topical gel preparation is **Sandrena®**. A prescription of **0.5 to 5 mg per day** can be appropriate (Seal 2007). The gel should be applied to the lower body (e.g. the thighs) each day. Gel should be applied to a different side of the body each day, to avoid irritation at the application site. Hands should be washed after application of the gel, and the area of application should not be washed for at least one hour after application.

---

6 Matrix patches have the medication embedded into the adhesive, while reservoir patches have a pool of medication behind a membrane which controls the release. Specific advice on whether a patch can be cut or not can be found at: www.remedysrxsp.ca/pdf/Transdermal_Patch.pdf

Implants

While estradiol has a history of being used in the form of an implant, this has been largely discontinued due to the availability of other delivery methods with more cost-effective manufacturing processes. Implants are also not recommended for trans people intending to undergo surgery but who have not yet done so, as they cannot be removed in the run-up to this.

Potential side effects of Estradiol

For detailed information on side effects, see the specific product information for the preparation being prescribed.

- weight gain

- headaches

- joint pain

- dizziness or nausea

- breast sensitivity/pain

- loss of fertility

- thromboembolism or deep vein thrombosis (DVT)

- impact on the liver (elevated enzymes)

- gallstones

- hyperprolactinaemia (high levels of prolactin in the blood – normal range is less than 20µg/L).[7]

---

7   Prolactin (a hormone released by the pituitary gland) levels can be higher in AFAB people – and especially spikes during pregnancy – due to its role in producing milk. High levels of prolactin may be associated with tumours on the pituitary gland. Endocrinological consultation may be necessary for management, with the possibility of treatment with bromocriptine, or other dopamine agonists.

GnRH analogues

For full information on GnRH analogues (such as goserelin), which can be used in the downregulation of testosterone in AMAB trans people, please see Chapter 6.

Antiandrogens

Antiandrogens are also known as testosterone blockers. They work by different mechanisms, either preventing the synthesis of the more potent dihydrotestosterone (DHT) from testosterone, or blocking testosterone from binding to androgen receptors. The different types of antiandrogens used in HRT are illustrated in the diagram below:

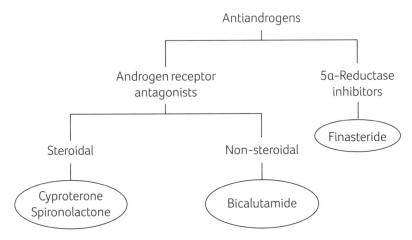

Figure 7.1: Diagram illustrating the varieties of antiandrogens commonly used in transgender patients.

Bicalutamide (Casodex®)

This antiandrogen is used by some clinicians in the United States, but is not used in the UK. Its primary use is in the treatment of prostate cancer, but may effectively block testosterone production at much lower doses than are given in that context. Bicalutamide is associated with some risk of liver function abnormalities (Kolvenbag and Blackledge 1996), which are deemed acceptable in the context of prostate cancer but less so in gender affirming medical intervention because of the range of other options available (Deutsch 2017).

Cyproterone (Androcur®, Cyprostat®, Dianette®)

Cyproterone can come as a preparation on its own (including Androcur® and Cyprostat®) or in combination with ethinylestradiol (Co-cyprindiol® and Dianette®). An oral dose of **50 to100 mg daily** is appropriate (Kreukels *et al.* 2014). Oral ethinylestradiol is no longer recommended for estrogen-based HRT due to increased risk of venous thrombosis and cardiovascular mortality (Asscheman *et al.* 2011), therefore cyproterone-only preparations are preferred.

Contraindications

- Allergic to cyproterone
- liver disease
- cancer (other than prostate)
- wasting diseases (unintended weight loss)
- blood clots (thrombosis or embolism).

Patients should discuss with their doctor before taking cyproterone if they have **diabetes mellitus**, **sickle cell anaemia**, or **depression**.

Spironolactone (Aldactone®)

Spironolactone is taken in tablet form, with a dose of **50 to 200 mg daily** being appropriate (Deutsch 2017). Combination preparations of spironolactone are available, but should not be used unless there are additional clinical reasons for the patient to receive the combined drug. **Aldactide®** is a combination of spironolactone with hydroflumethiazide (a diuretic), and **Lasilactone®** is a combination of spironolactone with furosemide (used to treat oedema or hypertension). Seal *et al.* (2012) showed that spironolactone use was associated with increased incidence of breast augmentation in trans women, while other antiandrogens (and GnRH analogues) were not. This may be because 'Spironolactone is a mineralocorticoid receptor antagonist that acts as an androgen receptor partial antagonist as well as an estrogen receptor agonist. As such, in addition to blocking the androgen receptor (which is its primary purpose in this situation), it also has a significant estrogenic action at the doses used in transwomen. One can postulate that this could lead to an excessive estrogenic action and consequent poorer breast outcome' (Seal *et al.* 2012, pp.4426). This implies that spironolactone use should be taken into account when a patient's estradiol dosage is being optimised.

Contraindications

- Allergic to spironolactone

- severe kidney problems or trouble urinating

- a diagnosis of Addison's disease

- hyperkalaemia (high potassium levels)

- a diagnosis of diabetes.

Finasteride (Proscar®)

Finasteride is a 5–alpha-reductase inhibitor, which prevents the conversion of testosterone to dihydrotestosterone (a more potent form). This is recommended for a limited time of prescription only (prior to GnRH analogue use) and can slow or stop male-pattern hair loss and body hair growth. Finasteride is taken as a tablet, with a dose of **1 to 5 mg daily** with UK-specific guidelines recommending 5 mg in the context of gender dysphoria (Greener 2014). Other branded finasteride preparations can be found (including **Aindeem®** and **Propecia®**) but these brands only come as 1 mg preparations. The most common side effects with finasteride are erectile dysfunction and breast swelling or tenderness – which may be desirable for some transfeminine people.

Any person taking finasteride who is having a sexual relationship with someone who has a possibility of becoming pregnant should avoid their partner being exposed to their semen (including skin contact), for as long as finasteride is taken. This is because if a person who is pregnant comes into contact with finasteride, this may cause foetal genital malformations.

Contraindications

- Allergic to finasteride

- assigned female at birth.

Testosterone

Testosterone is the most important male sex hormone, or androgen, although all people have some testosterone in their bodies. In the context of trans men and AFAB non-binary people, testosterone is often desired due to its role in masculinisation. The bodily changes are not an exact opposite of what is seen with estrogen treatment – for example, estrogen will not raise the voice, but testosterone will permanently lower it. The normal male range for testosterone is **10 to 30 nmol/L**. In the context of trans healthcare, dosing is a balance between increasing the trough serum testosterone to a male range, without seeing too much elevation in haematocrit. Contraindications and expected changes are listed below.

Contraindications for testosterone prescription

- Heart failure

- obstructive sleep apnea

- hormone-responsive breast cancer

- pregnancy

- unstable coronary artery disease

- untreated polycythemia[8] with a haematocrit of 55 per cent or higher.

---

8   This is when the volume of red blood cells in the blood (the haematocrit) is over 50 per cent, causing thick blood. This risk may be reduced via transdermal (patch) administration of testosterone.

Baseline tests prior to testosterone prescription

Blood pressure, full blood count, urea and electrolytes, liver function tests, fasting blood glucose or HbA1C (glycated haemoglobin), lipid profile, thyroid function, serum testosterone, estradiol, prolactin, LH, and FSH. For ongoing blood test monitoring, timing depends on the methods of testosterone delivery. Tests should be taken prior to injection on the day and then seven days later to gain trough and peak levels with monthly injections when necessary. For long-acting 3 month injections, tests should be taken two weeks prior and on the day before the injection, when necessary. Blood can be taken from a person using testosterone in gel four to six hours after application, ensuring no gel was administered on the arms (Seal 2007). Blood tests are advised to be done every four months for the first year, six-monthly for the following three years, and annually after that (Sunderland Clinical Commissioning Group 2014).

Table 7.2: Changes to be expected with testosterone

Bodily change:	First changes seen:	Little change expected after:	Reversibility
Increased oiliness of skin (potential for acne)	1 to 6 months	1 to 2 years	Reverts if testosterone stopped
Clitoral enlargement	1 to 6 months	1 to 2 years	Permanent
Periods stop	2 to 6 months	Continual with testosterone	Return if testosterone stopped
Vaginal atrophy and dryness	3 to 6 months	1 to 2 years	Reverts if testosterone stopped
Body fat redistribution	3 to 6 months	2 to 5 years	Reverts if testosterone stopped
Facial and body hair growth	3 to 6 months	3 to 5+ years	Permanent, would require electrolysis/ laser

Deeper voice	3 to 12 months	1 to 2 years	Permanent
Increased muscle mass and strength	3 to 12 months	2 to 5 years	Reverts if testosterone stopped
Male-pattern baldness onset (may be minimal or none)	>12 months	Variable	Halts if testosterone stopped, no regrowth

Different preparations, doses, and deliveries

Injections

Different types of testosterone injection are available – an injection every two to six weeks (beginning with greater frequency, every two to three weeks, is appropriate) with a dose of **150–250 mg**. **Testosterone Enantate** is available as a 250 mg/ml solution, as is the commonly used brand **Sustanon®** (which is a mix of esters). Trough serum testosterone and haematocrit should be used to guide each subsequent dose.

A longer acting injection with a loading phrase can be given approximately every three months (though potentially between 10 and 20 weeks, as needed), with a **1000 mg** dose. The most-used brand in the UK for this dose is **Nebido®** (available as a 1000 mg/4ml solution). Establishing a stable dose/interval for Nebido® can be more complex, and benefit from endocrinological referral.

Following a first injection (regardless of type), if on timing-appropriate follow-up a trough serum testosterone value of **8–12 nmol/L** is found, this is indicative of a good frequency. The next injection may be brought forward or delayed by one week depending on whether testosterone is at sub-therapeutic levels, or haematocrit is elevated, respectively. While the goal is to achieve steady-state serum testosterone, this can take three years with Nebido® and require extension of each injection interval to prevent an increased risk of polycythaemia (Sunderland Clinical Commissioning Group 2014). The peak serum testosterone should be approximately **25–30 nmol/L**.

Topical gel

The most common preparations are **Testogel®** or **Testim®** at doses of **50–100 mg daily**. Sachets are sometimes available but are being withdrawn – gel can also be prescribed as a pump dispenser. The equivalent to one sachet (the typical starting dose) is two squirts from the pump. A goal trough serum testosterone range of **15 to 20 nmol/L** is desirable, with the dose changed by 25 to 50 mg if necessary (increase if trough value is sub-therapeutic, decrease if haematocrit are elevated).

Capsules

Orally administered testosterone is available in the form of **Restandol® Testocaps™**. This is absorbed through the small intestine, avoiding the hepatotoxicity associated with older forms of oral testosterone (**C-17 alpha methylated testosterone**). However, this method of delivery means the testosterone is rapidly excreted, meaning that 3 to 6 capsules may be necessary each day, resulting in higher cost than other methods of delivery. As a result, this is not a commonly accessed source.

Potential side effects

- Acne
- local irritation at delivery site
- headaches
- dizziness
- hypertension
- increased blood pressure
- lipid derangements
- polycythemia.

Antiestrogens

While there are drugs which specifically have antiestrogenic effects (including several used in the treatment of breast cancer such as tamoxifen, anastrozole, and fulvestrant). These are rarely used as the masculinising impact of testosterone is less dependent on the downregulation of estrogen activity than vice-versa for AMAB trans people. In order to supress feminising secondary sexual characteristics, GnRH analogues (goserelin and leuprorelin) can be used – see Chapter 6 for full details.

Non-binary hormone regimens

It has been increasingly recognised that not all trans people wish to transition from their assignment at birth to the 'opposite gender' (Richards *et al.* 2016). What this means in the context of hormone prescription has, to date, lacked specific research. Among those non-binary people who experience gender dysphoria and wish to access hormones, identical treatment protocols to binary-oriented trans people of the same birth assignment is appropriate, as the same (or similar) bodily changes will assist with dysphoria – the difference is how the individual *conceptualises* their body. The subject of hormones (and surgeries) for non-binary people has been recently addressed in various chapters in the book *Genderqueer and Non-Binary Genders* (Richards *et al.* 2017).

Some people may feel more comfortable with low doses of estradiol or testosterone (though this may cause tiredness and reduced sex drive). This may simply result in the same changes happening to the body, but more slowly – however, significantly more research is needed in this area. This may be desirable or beneficial for a range of reasons, and does not eliminate the possibility of a more binary-oriented dose/transition pathway being followed over time. Some non-binary people may find that hormone access gives them the confidence to feel that they are 'trans enough', and shift to a more binary conceptualisation of themselves. Likewise the reverse is true – some people will approach transition presenting as within the gender binary, and later renegotiate themselves as non-binary (Vincent 2016).

It is important that clinicians do not assume that binary-oriented trans people have one discrete set of needs while non-binary trans people have another. Patients should be considered in an individual manner, such that a binary-oriented trans person might want a less typical transition pathway or a non-binary person might want a very traditional transition, without this undermining the reality of their experience of gender. Rigidity in gender transition pathways can be restrictive or harmful for all trans people. For example, until relatively recently is has been extremely rare for surgery to be accessible without significant time on a cross-sex hormone regimen. A non-binary person may desire mastectomy (for example) without taking testosterone. There is no medical reason why such a transition pathway cannot be followed, given the informed consent of the adult patient.

Some agender/non-gender people may desire a minimal hormone profile, where secondary sexual characteristics associated with being male *or* female are not expressed. There is no medical research on people taking blockers long term with no sex hormone supplementation. Inferences may be made from cases of androgen deficiency in cisgender men, and estrogen deficiency in cisgender women. Lower sex hormone levels are particularly associated with old age, or those who have the ovaries or testes removed without subsequent HRT. Risks and symptoms for people (regardless of birth assignment) with low testosterone and estrogen include libido loss, anxiety and depression, fatigue, hot flashes, headaches, insomnia, and osteoporosis. The importance of a sex hormone profile in the maintenance of bone health (Murphy *et al.* 1992) means that a permanent inhibition of all sex hormones may not be safe. However, the historical presence of eunuchs (AMAB people who had the testes removed with no hormonal replacement) does give some social precedent, although more research is certainly necessary.

Voice

While testosterone causes the voice to drop to a deeper pitch, estrogen does not affect the voice. Despite being therefore associated more with trans women, trans people of any birth assignment may benefit from vocal exercises to gradually make changes to the voice. Such changes include many dimensions in addition to the average pitch of speech. The different dimensions of **paralanguage** – the signals that we send with our voices other than the language we speak – also involves how we intone and emphasise, and the speed, volume, and resonance of speech (Mills and Stoneham 2017).

Vocal exercises may be used to masculinise, feminise, or neutralise the voice. Specific guidance on these exercises is beyond the scope of this book. More detailed guidance may be found in Matthew Mills' and Gillie Stoneham's book, *The Voice Book for Trans and Non-Binary People*.

Hair removal

Hair removal can be grouped into two categories – for the alleviation of dysphoria/increase in satisfaction of gendered appearance, and that which is necessary prior to some (genital) surgeries. Only electrolysis can be used for hair removal as part of surgical preparation, as this is 100 per cent effective and also works on hair of any colour. Risk of improper hair removal around the groin prior to surgery involves intra-vaginal or intra-urethral ingrown hairs which may result in infection. Arguments have been made that modern laser hair removal technology is effective or superior in hair removal for genital surgery (Zhang *et al.* 2016). Controlled clinical trials suggest that laser may be faster and less painful as a form of hair removal (Haedersdal and Wulf 2006), but laser cannot address lighter, blonde, or white hairs whilst electrolysis can.

Users of electrolysis or laser hair removal may find it significantly painful. **EMLA cream** may be prescribed as local anaesthesia, which must be applied one hour before an appointment, and allowed to sit and absorb into the skin without being rubbed. Lidocaine jelly or lidocaine/prilocaine cream are other pain management prescription options (Thomas and Unger 2017).

Electrolysis

The process of electrolysis involves using a probe to deliver electricity to individual hair follicles. There are three different types of electrolysis, but all involve the same treatment experience. A qualified electrologist inserts a metal probe as thin as a human hair into each hair follicle, one at a time (this does not break the skin). The **Galvanic Method** causes sodium hydroxide to form in the follicle, killing it. The **Thermolytic Method** heats the hair follicle, essentially cauterising the blood supply. The **Blend Method** combines these applications. Trans accounts anecdotally suggest that the galvanic method is more effective at killing the hairs permanently, but the thermolytic method may remove more hairs per session (James 2017). Ultimately the experience of electrolysis is subjective, with no method showing a clear advantage over another. The most important factor is the correct application of the electrologist. Service users seeking electrolysis are advised to use a member of the **British Institute and Association of Electrolysis** (BIAE) to ensure the training and skill of the practitioner.

Laser hair removal

Laser hair removal functions by monochromatic light selectively heating melanin. This is why laser is more effective the darker and coarser the hair being removed. Light is refracted down the length of the hair to cauterise the follicle. Cauterisation may be partial, which is why a hair may grow back but 'weaker' than before, and require multiple sessions over the same area to achieve a result (Olsen 1999). Newer laser technology is capable of targeting the melanin in the root of the hair without dispersing to the melanin in surrounding skin, if the person seeking hair removal is not white.

Intense Pulsed Light (IPL) Hair Removal is similar to laser, but uses a broader spectrum of wavelength. It has been shown that diode lasers are overall more effective, more painful, and less time-consuming than IPL (Klein *et al.* 2013). IPL is effective for hair reduction, but not complete and permanent hair removal. When compared to electrolysis, more hairs can be covered per session.

Binding

This is the practice where AFAB people may flatten the chest to create a more masculine chest appearance. Binding may be possible regardless of the size of the chest. This may sometimes be done to some extent using a sports bra, swimming costume, or sports compression wear worn under clothing. Others may use 'DIY' methods such as binding with ACE™ bandages, or even duct tape or plastic wrap. Purpose-designed binders may also be purchased[9].

---

9   For reviews of recommended binder brands, please see here: https://www.
    bustle.com/p/11-of-the-best-binders-you-can-buy-according-to-a-trans-
    person-30921

An analysis of 1800 trans people who bind their chest provides some insights into the health impacts of the different forms of binding (Peitzmeier *et al.* 2017). From the sample, one of the most severe health outcomes from binding was rib fractures, which was only associated with binding with bandages or athletic compression wear. ACE™ bandages constrict in response to movement to provide support for injuries, and so breathing with a bandage-bound chest may place strain on the ribcage. The statistical analysis by Peitzmeier *et al.* is limited for judging the 'overall safety' of different binding methods because of the differences in subpopulation sample sizes. That a wider *range* of negative health outcomes were reported for commercial binders than for duct tape does not indicate that commercial binders are less safe, when we consider that 1570 participants used binders, but only 78 used duct tape or plastic wrap. The study supports the often-repeated advice within transmasculine communities that ACE™ bandage, tape, or plastic wrap are likely the riskiest forms of binding. The use of binders is associated with various forms of discomfort such as sweating (which may contribute to back acne if also taking testosterone), itchiness, numbness, headaches, shortness of breath, or fatigue. These may be potentially small, or considered acceptable in the alleviation of gender dysphoria.

Over half of the sample in Peitzmeier *et al.*'s study bind seven days a week. Many transmasculine people may feel uncomfortable to ever not bind, or leave a binder on during sleep. Long-term binding may affect the elasticity of skin, which may have ramifications for top surgery. This would not prevent someone from accessing surgery, but may impact what final results are possible, and aesthetic satisfaction. Taking days off from binding (if not going out, for example) or avoiding wearing a binder for over 8 hours at a time is advisable. It is also important if using a commercially available binder to use an appropriate size, as not only will a binder that is too small be more uncomfortable, but may push the chest to the sides and give a less effective bind.

Tucking

For trans people assigned male at birth who have a penis, tucking is the act of positioning the penis and testes down and back to avoid any 'bulge' of the crotch. Depending on the individual, some people may move the testes out of the scrotum into the abdomen (into the inguinal canal), while others push them between the legs with the penis. This can have ramifications for fertility, because sperm quality and quantity is optimised at a cooler temperature than inside the body, and tucking can cause the testes to overheat. Warmth and sweating from tucking can create vulnerability for skin infections, so it can be important to not tuck constantly.

Two of the most common methods of tucking include using sports tape to hold the penis back, or the use of a **gaff** – underwear or a 'holster' to help push the penis and testes back. The former method may give greater security and stability, but also means one cannot urinate without undoing and redoing the tuck.[10]

Prostheses

Whether used while waiting for surgery or as a consistent or occasional alternative, many trans people benefit from a reduction in dysphoria by using anatomically specific products to create differences in body shape (which can assist with 'passing'). These include **packers**[11], prosthetic penises, **stand-to-pee (STP) devices**[12], **breast forms**[13], and **body padding**[14]. These might simply aid in the relationship with oneself and confidence, or with specific activities such as urination (with STPs) or sexual activity (with certain types of packer that can have a rod inserted to allow them to function as an erect penis). Trans people are advised not to use methods (such as glue) that may cause skin damage, as this can compromise later surgeries.

---

10 Guidance on both methods and consideration of health can be found here: www.buzzfeed.com/meredithtalusan/all-the-questions-you-had-about-tucking-but-were-afraid-to-a?utm_term=.wlZ0r1oL8#.xm9en96xJ

11 For more information about packers, please see: ftm-guide.com/guide-to-packers-for-transmen

12 For more information about STPs, please see: transguys.com/features/stp

13 For more information on breast forms, please see: transgenderuniverse.com/2016/05/24/breast-forms

14 For more information on padding, please see: transhealth.phsa.ca/social-transition-options/binding-packing-tucking/padding

Gamete storage

Taking hormones is known to negatively impact fertility, therefore some trans people may wish to store sperm or eggs. There is no evidence to suggest that trans status has any impact on a person's suitability or capability as a parent (White and Ettner 2007, Richards and Seal 2014). GICs should give advice on gamete storage before HRT is started, but gamete storage is not always available on the NHS, and depends upon local fertility services which can be found here: https://www.hfea.gov.uk/i-am/fertility-preservation

Chapter 8

Gender Affirmation Surgeries

This chapter will look at surgical interventions used to help trans people with gender dysphoria. The chapter provides a brief overview of different forms of surgery available for restructuring secondary sex characteristics or the genitals and gonads as part of gender transition. Regret associated with trans surgical interventions is also reviewed, due to being considerably lower than many may assume or fear, and intimately connected to how trans people experience the healthcare system rather than transition being fundamentally inappropriate.

This chapter does not go into technical detail on how surgeries are performed, as technical instruction of surgical specialists is beyond the scope of this book. Further to this, no photographs of pre- or post-surgical results are shown. Generalisations about surgical results should not be drawn from single images (particularly as the subject of the image may have differences in morphology or desired outcomes compared to the viewer). As a result, anything less than a comparative gallery of different people is not likely to be very helpful for any readers considering whether a procedure might be right for them. Such galleries are often available on the websites of private surgeons, which can also give insights into that individual practitioner's specialisms. Additionally, in the context of medical literature there has been a history of unnecessary and voyeuristic photography of trans and intersex bodies (particularly children), often without consent, which has not provided explicit educational purpose (Creighton *et al.* 2002).

Surgeries that modify the breast/chest area may be collectively referred to as 'top surgery', while surgeries performed on the genital area are correspondingly 'bottom surgery'. These terms are well established and understood within trans communities.

Referral for surgery

Surgical referrals are done by the GIC, not by GPs. Trans people have choice over which surgeon they would like to be referred to. Therefore it is worthwhile for trans people to investigate what procedures available surgeons do, and what specialisms they have. Surgeons associate higher risk in patients who have a BMI over 30. Larger amounts of fat can increase the risk of clots or post-surgical infections, and make the location of blood vessels more difficult. Stopping smoking is strongly advisable, particularly in advance of genital surgery. It is standard for surgeons to require that patients have stopped smoking for at least six months prior to genital surgical interventions (Christopher *et al.* 2017).

Chest reconstruction – general information

In patients taking HRT, there is no need for this to be stopped prior to surgery. While both estrogen and testosterone are associated with risk of blood clots (such that cessation prior to bottom surgery is necessary), the fact that patients can stand and walk immediately post-surgically renders this a low enough risk to not merit stopping hormones (Yelland 2017).

The results of top surgery can also be negatively affected by significant amounts of postoperative weight loss. Stability in weight is recommended to ensure the results of surgery are not affected.

Top surgery for trans men and AFAB non-binary people

Following referral (done by the GIC), patients will receive an examination by the surgeon during a consultation, to assess what surgical intervention is desired and/or suitable. Factors that are considered include ptosis (droop), nipple position, and skin elasticity (Yelland 2017). Mammogram should be offered to all patients as a precaution, if desired. Patients should note that even with mastectomy, this does not completely eliminate the possibility of breast cancer, but does significantly lower the risk (post-surgical risk is similar to cisgender men, who can, in rare cases, also contract breast cancer). Breast cancer in a post-mastectomy trans man has previously been reported (Nikolic *et al.* 2012).

The nipple has a complex nerve supply, which is often affected in masculinising chest surgery, with loss of sensation possible. Only small sample sizes are available with post-operative feedback, but in a sample with 12 trans respondents, 7 retained nipple sensitivity (Nelson *et al.* 2009). Loss of sensitivity is more likely if the areolae are resized, or if the nipples' positions need to be relocated.

Bilateral mastectomy – double incision

This is the most common surgical method for breast tissue removal in trans people. Incisions are made at the crease of each breast, or slightly under. The nipple-areolar complex (NAC) is removed as a skin graft to be repositioned to give a masculine phenotype. Note, a small amount of glandular and fatty tissue is left behind to maintain the contour of the pectoral.

Characteristic bilateral scarring is produced from the double incision technique, which whiten and fade over time. Scarring also varies significantly between different people. Healing of scar tissue can be aided by the use of silicone gel strips (SGSs) post-surgery (Bleasdale *et al.* 2015). Some patients may experience pouching of skin towards the armpits, or towards the middle of the chest. Particularly if small, skin may naturally shift over time and not require correction. In some cases, a revision surgery may be performed to excise excess skin.

While the double incision technique is the most common mastectomy method, the **buttonhole technique** and **inverted T technique** have also been developed. These methods hope (but do not guarantee) to preserve nipple sensitivity with more frequency and efficacy. This is weighed against association with less chest flatness, restrictions on the position of the NAC, and limitations in how much muscular definition may later be achieved[1]. The availability of choice will depend upon the individual surgeon, and what techniques they are willing and able to deploy.

Post-surgery, some surgeons may use drains to remove fluid build-up (seroma), but this is dependent on practitioner preference and is not standardised. Different forms of stitching may be used.

Periareolar surgery

This method is only effective when the breast volume is already particularly small (approximately 150g of material to be removed from each breast, or less). This method involves little movement of the nipple. A doughnut shaped section of skin is removed around the areolae, leaving the nipple attached in the location of the 'hole' of the doughnut. Glandular tissue is removed, and the skin drawn in and sutured to the nipple edge (often reducing the areolae to a male-pattern size of approximately 22 mm). Excess skin may result in 'puckering' around the nipple, which may require revision. The double incision technique is generally viewed as giving a tight and smooth chest. On the other hand, the periareolar technique leaves comparably minimal scarring, and is associated with high preservation of nipple sensitivity. For patients with minimal breast tissue **keyhole surgery** may be possible, which uses only a small incision under the bottom half of each nipple.

Liposuction

The breast is comprised of fatty tissue, and glandular tissue. For the most part, liposuction will not produce an adequately masculine chest due to the remaining glandular tissue which liposuction does not remove, but this may be an appropriate method for breast reduction (for a non-binary person, for example) rather than complete removal.

---

1   More information about the pros and cons of buttonhole and inverted T chest surgery are available here: https://www.genderconfirmation.com/surgery/buttonhole

Top surgery for trans women and AMAB non-binary people

Trans women and transfeminine non-binary people who take estrogen are recommended to wait at least 12 months from first prescription to allow for breast development before deciding whether additional augmentation is necessary or desirable. It should be recognised that some trans people may wish to access surgery without HRT, and so hormone prescription should not be viewed as a prerequisite for surgical referral, assessment, or access.

Breast implants

Implants can be placed either beneath any glandular breast tissue present, or deeper, beneath the pectoralis major muscle. Accessing HRT after breast augmentation surgery has not been well studied. Most surgeons use the crease underneath where the breast sits (or will sit) as the incision site as this effectively hides scarring, although other incision sites are possible.

Different types of breast implants are possible. Variation can be in terms of shape, size, texture, and material. After breast augmentation, it is common to experience pain and sound – caused by trapped air which will be harmlessly absorbed (after several days), and tenderness and swelling (for several weeks). Psychosocial wellbeing is likely to significantly improve after surgery (Weigert et al. 2013) though extensive, specific research has not been conducted.

Anyone with breast tissue may wish to access a mammogram in the event of finding a concerning lump. It should be noted that mobile screening units may not use equipment with sharp enough resolution to create diagnostically useful images where a person has breast implants (which are visible on mammograms), and will need to access a hospital department (Phillips et al. 2014).

Following breast augmentation long-term, there can be different reasons for another operation to be needed. Scar tissue that forms around an implant (called the capsule) can contract over time, which may negatively affect the shape of the breast, and create a harder, and tender area. This isn't a dangerous concern, however Yelland (an experienced UK breast/chest surgeon) reports a risk of 'notable firmness' as 'approximately seven per cent [of patients] at the five-year mark' (Yelland 2017, p.259). Implants also have a very small risk of leakage, which may not necessarily be noticed due to containment by scar tissue. Breast implant manufacturers also often have guarantees on their products covering a length of time (usually ten years), which may be checked with the surgeon if concerned.

Vocal surgery to raise pitch

Possibly the most widely known form of vocal surgery for transfeminine people is **cricothyroid approximation**, where the goal is increased tension of the vocal folds. It may be possible for this surgery to be arranged at the same time as a thyroid chondroplasty, depending on the surgeon and funding. Evidence suggests that cricothyroid approximation can provide benefits for some patients (Yang *et al.* 2002), but that pitch elevation alone may not result in a voice being socially regarded as 'feminine' (Van Borsel *et al.* 2008). Reports have also been made where cricothyroid approximation may result in a loss of ability to raise pitch to pre-surgical levels, and reductions in range, control, and volume, even if pitch was maintained at a higher average (Freidenberg 2002). It is also possible for patients to experience a gradual drop in pitch over time post-surgery[2]. Other methods that may be used for vocal feminisation include **Wendler glottoplasty** (Mastronikolis *et al.* 2013) and **Laser-Assisted Voice Adjustment (LAVA)** (Orloff *et al.* 2006). These surgeries are not (currently) available in the UK, therefore this information is included for the sake of completion, and the benefit of international readers or trans people who may seek private healthcare in other countries.

Facial feminisation surgeries

This is the collective term for a range of different surgical procedures to the face and neck, to create an appearance that

---

2   Discussion of cricothyroid approximation by a surgeon, together with pre- and post-surgical recordings can be found here: https://www.voicedoctor. net/surgery/pitch/cricothyroid-approximation

allows the individual to be socially read as female/feminine more easily. Facial feminisation surgery may be abbreviated to FFS. During pre-surgical consultation, there are different forms of imaging that may be used to analyse facial structures, depending on procedures which may be desired or recommended. Types of imaging include **cone beam computerised tomography** (CBCT) for imaging the frontal sinus, or an **orthopantomogram** (OPG) to image the chin and jaw, as with a dental X-ray. **Photography** may also be requested.

The fact that movement is not restricted following surgery means that hormone regimens do not need to be stopped for any facial feminisation surgery – however countermeasures may be provided to minimise risk of blood clots (including compression stockings/boots, and/or low molecular weight heparin). Most surgeries require one or two nights in hospital, and several weeks off from work.

Reshaping the forehead

Potential patients should note that shaving of the hair is not necessary for procedures of the forehead or scalp. Surgical discussions of specific techniques – and their alignment with good patient satisfaction – have been published (Capitán *et al.* 2014). Contouring of 'frontal bossing' due to a large frontal sinus or thick supra-orbital ridges is common (Altman 2012). Simultaneous hair transplantation may also potentially be managed in a single procedure (Capitán *et al.* 2017).

Brow lift

This procedure raises the resting position of the eyebrows. This may be complemented by removal of loose skin around the eyes if appropriate (Altman 2017). Detailed case studies of procedures found satisfactory have been published (Cho and Jin 2012). Pain and bruising around the eyes is common following a brow lift. Patients are also advised not to blow their nose for 10 days post-procedure, as this could push air through the frontal sinuses (behind the brow ridges) and place the healing area under strain.

Hairline advance

It has been claimed that a typical feminine hairline position is approximately 5 to 6 cm above a point between the top of the nose and the eyebrows (Mayer and Fleming 1985), but it is important to highlight that individual happiness and comfort is of central importance, and that women have a wide range of possible hairlines which they are satisfied with. Movement of the hairline can depend on scalp laxity (stretchiness of the skin). If this is insufficient, there is precedent for the use of expanders to be temporarily inserted under the skin, and inflated with silicone over time to strategically stretch the skin in preparation for surgical hairline advancement (Adson *et al.* 1987, Manders *et al.* 1984). Post-surgical care involves keeping the scalp clean by washing with normal shampoo and conditioner.

Lip lift

Unlike virtually all other forms of gender affirming surgery, a lip lift may be performed under local anaesthesia (if done alone – though may be combined with other more involved surgical interventions). This involves the removal of tissue between the bottom of the nose and the top of the lip, which can help curl the upper lip slightly upwards. This can also allow more show of the teeth when smiling. Surgical techniques continue to be refined, however disruption of the nasal sill (the area directly underneath the nostrils) is regarded as a problem only minimised through surgical skill (Raphael *et al.* 2014).

Rhinoplasty – nose job

This is a common surgery among cisgender people, and is among the least specialised forms of FFS. One of the most controversial complexities in facial feminisation surgery is the codification of phenotypic variation as closer to or further from masculine or feminine 'ideals'. This is most apparent in the literature around rhinoplasties which may make reference to the 'feminine nose' (Spiegel 2017). Patients may wish for a particularly small (or button) nose which may be imbalanced with the rest of the face, therefore reflection on expectations and overall result is advised. Cho (2017) draws attention to the importance of recognising the impact of white-centric beauty norms on surgical guidance, such that race/ethnicity are taken into account with non-white recipients of rhinoplasty (Rohrich and Bolden 2010). Various alterations may be done with a rhinoplasty including a narrowing or straightening of the bridge, and nostril size reduction.

Cheek implants

The implants used are made of high density polyethylene, with different sizes and shapes possible. There are differences in surgical opinion regarding the value of removing fat pads in the cheeks to produce 'hollowing' (Altman 2017). Some patients may experience numbness in the upper half of the mouth, but sensation most often returns over time.

Genioplasty – chin reduction

Such a procedure involves the narrowing and shortening of the chin through bone removal, via the mouth. Due to post-surgical pain, bruising, and swelling, a soft or liquid diet may be beneficial for several days. As comparable with cheek surgery there may be numbness which is likely to dissipate over several weeks. The use of a germicidal mouthwash for several weeks post-surgery in addition to tooth-brushing will help maintain a cleaner environment for wound healing.

Jaw shave

An angular jaw shape is socially coded as more masculine, such that contouring may benefit some transfeminine people. Due to extensive modification of the jaw bone, postoperative pain and bruising can be expected for several weeks, and swelling and stiffness for several months. Similar mouth care to a chin reduction procedure may assist with wound healing.

Tracheal shave

Also technically called **thyroid chondroplasty** or **chondro-laryngoplasty**, this involves the removal of prominent cartilage (the 'Adam's apple') from the front of the neck.

The consistency of thyroid cartilage is age-dependent, becoming harder over time through ossification (turning into bone). A rare side-effect in younger people accessing this surgery can be for the vocal cords to shift if the cartilage structure is weakened, which can cause voice pitch to become lower. As with the voice generally, coaching or surgery are potential options if this happens. Whilst unlikely, this is even more improbable in older people because of the additional strength of the (bonier) supporting structures.

Genital surgeries for trans women and AMAB non-binary people

Practitioners should note that even in cases where a transfeminine person wishes to access genital surgery, this does not always mean vaginoplasty is desired. Further, different techniques and results of vaginoplasty are available. In particular, vaginal construction may be done with reduced depth (not enough for penetrative sex) which reduces the risk of complications and makes surgical recovery easier – or a vulva and clitoris can be constructed without a vagina (Selvaggi and Andreasson 2017).

Orchidectomy

Also sometimes spelled orchiectomy, is the removal of the testes. Recently, specific techniques of orchidectomy have been reported for specific deployment in trans people (rather than cisgender men with testicular cancer), which takes into account the potential for future or concurrent vaginoplasty (Washington *et al.* 2017). Many transfeminine people will have an orchidectomy at the same time as vaginoplasty rather than as separate procedures, but some may desire testicular removal while leaving the penis. Orchidectomy removes the source of endogenous testosterone, ending any need for antiandrogen therapy. Estradiol would however continue to be taken as normal, for those trans people who have accessed hormones.

Vaginoplasty

The most common construction of a vagina uses inverted penile skin – **penile inversion vaginoplasty** (Perovic *et al.* 2000). An alternative uses a segment of the bowel (**total laparoscopic sigmoid vaginoplasty**) which can be necessary if there is a lack of tissue to use to create the vagina (Bouman *et al.* 2016). This may be if a patient has been circumcised and/or has a small penis, (particularly common if the patient has accessed puberty blockers at Tanner Stage 2 or 3). Due to involvement of the abdomen this may be regarded as a more involved surgery (with associated risks), but also has advantages of less postoperative dilation needed, greater depth, and self-lubrication (Deutsch 2016). In rarer cases, vaginoplasty has been performed using skin grafts from donor sites (Hage and Karim 1998). The narrower an individual's pelvis, the greater the potential difficulty of creating adequate vaginal width. The labia majora are typically constructed from scrotal skin.

One of the most commonly reported post-surgical complications is **vaginal stenosis**, where the new vaginal passage narrows and/or shortens (Horbach *et al.* 2015). A dilation regimen is necessary to maintain vaginal depth and width over time[3]. A **fistula**[4] is an uncommon but serious risk, potentially occurring between the vagina and the anus, the vagina and the urethra, or the vagina and the pouch of Douglas (part of the abdominal cavity). A retrospective study indicated that out of 1,082 trans women who received 1,037 vaginoplasties and 80 revision surgeries, there were 25 cases of fistula formation (13 rectovaginal, 11 urethrovaginal, and 1 pouch-vaginal), giving a 2.2 per cent incidence rate (Van Der Sluis *et al.* 2016). However rectovaginal fistula was more likely in revision surgery (5/80 vs. 8/1037), suggesting a lower incidence rate among trans people having a primary vaginoplasty.

Postoperative care may see spotting of blood from the vagina (or more significant bleeding) during dilation, which may need treatment with silver nitrate, or local excision of granulated

---

3   Guidance on a dilation regimen should be provided by the surgeon, and will initially be multiple times per day, reducing over time. Informal guidance from the transfeminine community on dilation may be found here: www.tsroadmap.com/physical/vaginoplasty/dilation.html

4   An abnormal connection, essentially a hole between two hollow areas which should not be there.

scar tissue (Thomas and Unger 2017). A brown or yellow vaginal discharge should be expected for the first four to six weeks following surgery, and hygiene may be assisted by douching using soap and water (Deutsch 2016). Postoperative oversensitivity of the clitoris may also be experienced by some, but this is likely to settle. In one recent study 19 out of 22 participants had experienced clitoral orgasm post-surgery (Sigurjónsson *et al.* 2017).

While not yet available, the possibility of uterus transplants for trans women in the future has been considered (Murphy 2015). Uterus transplantation in cis women is still experimental, although has resulted in successful births.

Genital surgeries for trans men and AFAB non-binary people

Physical examination is typically conducted at a first surgical consultation, in order to assess what type of surgery is wanted, and in the case of phalloplasty, potential donor site options.

Salpingo-Oophorectomy and hysterectomy

Salpingo-Oophorectomy is the removal of the fallopian tubes and ovaries, and hysterectomy is the removal of the uterus. Hysterectomy may be **laparoscopic** (keyhole surgery) vaginal, or **abdominal**, with the latter resulting in more scarring. Total vaginal hysterectomy is where the uterus is removed via the vagina, and this has been demonstrated as a viable technique for trans men (Obedin-Maliver *et al.* 2014). Different types of hysterectomy are possible. The most common for AFAB trans people is a **radical hysterectomy**, as this removes the uterus, cervix, ovaries, and fallopian tubes. A **total hysterectomy** removes just the uterus and cervix, and a **partial hysterectomy** removes only the uterus, but leaves the cervix in place.

Metoidioplasty

This is a significantly less major surgery compared to phalloplasty, and can give a pleasing aesthetic result. Metoidioplasty is only possible following testosterone use, as the procedure depends upon the engorgement of the clitoris. By separating the clitoris from the labia minora and releasing the suspensory ligament, the clitoris can be repositioned to visually function as a phallus. Phallic engorgement from testosterone treatment is usually limited to a maximum size of 4 to 6 cm (2 to 3 inches), and therefore is unlikely to allow for postoperative insertive sexual penetration. However, sexual sensitivity is often well-preserved, and the urethra can be repositioned to allow for urination while standing (Djordjevic *et al.* 2009). In the construction of the urethra, a graft is likely to be taken from inside the cheek (Djordjevic and Bizic 2013). **Vaginectomy** (removal of the vaginal cavity) and **scrotoplasty** (construction of a scrotum) are commonly performed at the same time as a metoidioplasty but are not essential. It is possible to later access phalloplasty if a metoidioplasty has already been accessed.

Phalloplasty

A phalloplasty is one of several forms of surgery used to construct a penis for a transmasculine person. One of the earliest phalloplastic constructions was performed in 1936 by Nikolaj Bogoraz, using tube skin grafts with implanted rib cartilage (Bergman *et al.* 1948, Schultheiss *et al.* 2005). The **Pedicled Tube** procedure was the oldest form of phalloplasty, but was significantly limited in sensation, function, and appearance, and also required multiple surgeries. Chang and Hwang (1984) pioneered the **Free Flap** procedure, where tissue is removed from the forearm with a section of radial artery, and the blood vessels are reattached at the new site. Free flap procedures have been developed that use donor tissue from other sites, including the thigh, the side of the chest or back, the lower leg, or the upper arm and shoulder.

A **Local Flap** procedure uses tissue donated from the abdomen or pubic region, and differs from a free flap procedure because the blood supply is never severed – the donor tissue is rotated into position. A **Pedicled Flap** procedure using tissue from the inner thigh is another method (Descamps *et al.* 2009), but in a recent comparison with forearm free flap surgery was associated with greater risk of postoperative complication (Ascha *et al.* 2017). It is recognised that a disparity exists between the research done on AFAB bottom surgery options and improvements, with significant need for higher quality data and innovation (Frey *et al.* 2017). Significant scarring, slow healing, sensory changes and loss of strength are associated with donation sites (Selvaggi *et al.* 2006). Patients should discuss with their surgeon what options are available, and what the potential benefits and drawbacks of different options may be in the context of their individual anatomy and physiology.

The donor site for a phalloplasty needs to be relatively (but not perfectly) hairless, as hairs in the new urethra can cause significant problems (Christopher *et al.* 2017). Time for hair removal may therefore need to be taken into account, as well as time to ensure that hair regrowth is minimal prior to a surgery being booked.

Trans men may wish to have two silicone prosthetic testes inserted into the constructed scrotum, though some may wish one of those to be substituted for a pump to facilitate erection of the new penis. This is inserted in the scrotum at the same time as an inflatable cylinder is included in the penis, and a reservoir filled with fluid in the abdomen. The pump can be pressed to move fluid from the reservoir to the penis to allow erection, and reversed to return to a flaccid state.

In addition to the BMI restriction of less than 30, some phalloplastic surgeons may require a minimum BMI due to the necessity of subcutaneous fat to provide bulk to the phallus. Christopher *et al.* (2017) explain they generally set a minimum BMI requirement of 18, but are also aware of the importance of individual assessment and so do make exceptions (where someone has a high BMI due to being very muscular, or a low BMI due to a significant lack of muscle, but with levels of body fat that do not create surgical issues).

Postoperative care in the community for a free flap phalloplasty involves the changing of donor site dressings (a silicone sheet) by a nurse practitioner. Salt baths for 10 to 15 minutes for the donor area are advised every couple of days to help keep the area clean (Christopher *et al.* 2017).

Regret associated with surgeries

Surgical regret is recognised as being extremely small among the trans population. This is consistent across transfeminine people and transmasculine people (Lawrence 2003, Morrison *et al.*

2016, Pfafflin 1993, Rachlin *et al.* 2010, Sigurjónsson *et al.* 2017, Vujovic *et al.* 2009). This does not mean regret does not exist, as it does for all medical interventions. A study assessing every case of reassignment surgery performed in Sweden between 1960 and 2010 found the percentage of patients experiencing any regret totalled 2.2 per cent (a total of 5 AFAB and 10 AMAB people). Regret *also* significantly declined over time within the sample, which may be attributed to a complex combination of declining social stigma and increased legal protections, more nuanced and sensitive practitioner approaches, and developments to improve the experiences and outcomes of surgery (Dhejne *et al.* 2014).

The reasons that can underpin experiences of regret can involve significantly under-recognised complexity, and not be simply the result of an unsure patient given inappropriate access. For example, Rachlin *et al.* (2010) surveyed 134 trans men who had oophorectomy and hysterectomy, with six of the men answering 'yes' to the question 'do you have any regrets about having had your reproductive organ surgery'. It is vital to note that *all* of these men clarified that having the procedure was the right decision for them, but regrets included wishing they'd done it sooner, wishing they'd used another surgeon or had a different type of procedure, or wished they hadn't experienced loss of sexual sensation as a side effect.

A detailed case study has been written on one particular case of regret regarding vaginoplasty, conducted in 1987 (Olsson and Möller 2006). While the report goes into great detail about the difficult life of the subject, the absolute failure of contemporary medical assessment to appreciate the possibility of a non-binary gender identity may have contributed to the patient's unsatisfactory experience. The authors describe the patient's gender identity by saying 'sometimes she felt like neither a man nor a woman but like a neuter, while at other times she had the feeling of being an individual with two sexes' (Olsson and Möller 2006, p.505) while also describing themselves as feeling they had both a man and a woman within themselves. That the patient was not 'a cisgender person who was misdiagnosed' is supported by the fact that they continued taking estrogen long-term post-surgery, did not revise their legal change of sex, and were pleased with the results of facial epilation – indicative of various forms of treatment or social change being well-received.

Concluding Remarks

This book has been an ambitious project. I've attempted to bring together the best possible medical evidence in the provision of trans healthcare while ensuring that language is both clear and respectful, and able to be operationalised within current healthcare policy. It is important to recognise that both of these domains – language and policy – tend to shift over time, and risk making parts of the book obsolete. This will hopefully be addressed either in future editions, or by a new generation of trans experts. For practitioners who have read this book, either in its entirety or particular sections, my hope is that several key themes will underscore their medical practice with trans people. Firstly, to echo Dr. John Dean (of The Laurels Gender Identity Clinic): trans people are, first and foremost, people. We deserve respect, empathy, and reflexivity. By reflexivity, I mean the practice of scrutinising ourselves, checking for unjustified predilections, and being open to learning from the people we encounter.

Secondly, that despite the amount of detail that it is possible to go into, the provision of trans healthcare is not overwhelmingly complex (in the vast majority of cases). It is understandable that practitioners may feel concerned or uncertain about being asked to provide this kind of care, given how little (if any) trans-specific healthcare training is given as part of a UK doctor's medical education. Further, it is arguably unfair that practitioners must assume full legal responsibility when providing a prescription, regardless of context. While this works well for the majority of medical practice, this opens a discrepancy between how 'informed consent' is viewed in clinical practice and the trans community. For the former, informed consent means that a doctor must secure informed agreement from a patient before starting them on a treatment, and that consent can be withdrawn if the patient doesn't agree with the doctor's plan of action. Essentially, a patient who understands the risks can opt out of a doctor's treatment plan. The informed consent model of trans healthcare, however, means that when a trans person asks for, say, HRT – and they understand the potential risks, what can be expected, and so on – the doctor should not refuse, but *also* that the doctor cannot be held accountable should the person receiving treatment later regret it (and claim the practitioner should have stopped them). This would remove the pressure on doctors to act as gatekeepers, and place full agency in the hands of the trans person. Of course, few trans people are medical doctors – though it's important to recognise that a substantial number of trans people have exceptional knowledge of trans healthcare, exceeding that of the majority of practitioners. Even under such a system, guidance, support, and competent practice are still absolutely needed. The UK's current system is no longer fit for purpose, as GICs simply cannot see their patients in a reasonable time frame. I believe the most plausible solution will be similar to Canadian practice, where (in short) hormone provision is managed entirely in primary care, and trans people are only referred to GICs when pursuing specialist surgery. How this might be operationalised is a key future point to be negotiated.

Finally, trans people are not just patients. We are colleagues, friends, family, children, parents, lovers. Maybe we are yours, or a key part of the life of someone you know. There is so much more to being trans than healthcare provision. Remembering that can help us to connect, and remember that trans healthcare should never be adversarial.

References

Adamus, M., Gabrhelik, T., & Marek, O. (2008). Influence of gender on the course of neuromuscular block following a single bolus dose of cisatracurium or rocuronium. *European journal of anaesthesiology, 25*(7), 589-595.

Adson, M. H., Anderson, R. D., & Argenta, L. C. (1987). Scalp expansion in the treatment of male pattern baldness. *Plastic and reconstructive surgery, 79*(6), 906-914.

Ålgars, M., Alanko, K., Santtila, P., & Sandnabba, N. K. (2012). Disordered eating and gender identity disorder: a qualitative study. *Eating disorders, 20*(4), 300-311.

Altman, K. (2012). Facial feminization surgery: current state of the art. *International journal of oral and maxillofacial surgery, 41*(8), 885-894.

Altman, K. (2017). Facial Feminization Surgery. In W. P. Bouman & J. Arcelus (Eds.), *The Transgender Handbook* (pp. 301-317). New York: Nova Science Publishers.

American Geriatrics Society Ethics Committee. (2015). American Geriatrics Society care of lesbian, gay, bisexual, and transgender older adults position statement: American Geriatrics Society Ethics Committee. *Journal of the American Geriatrics Society, 63*(3), 423-426.

American Psychiatric Association. (2013). *Diagnostic and Statistical Manual of Mental Disorders* (5th ed.). Arlington, VA: American Psychiatric Association.

Ansara, Y. G. & Hegarty, P. (2014). Methodologies of misgendering: Recommendations for reducing cisgenderism in psychological research. *Feminism & Psychology, 24*(2), 259-270.

Ascha, M., Massie, J. P., Morrison, S. D., Crane, C. N., & Chen, M. L. (2018). Outcomes of single stage phalloplasty by pedicled anterolateral thigh flap versus radial forearm free flap in gender confirming surgery. *The Journal of Urology, 199*(1), 206-214.

Asscheman, H., Giltay, E. J., Megens, J. A., van Trotsenburg, M. A., & Gooren, L. J. (2011). A long-term follow-up study of mortality in transsexuals receiving treatment with cross-sex hormones. *European journal of endocrinology, 164*(4), 635-642.

Austin, A. & Craig, S. L. (2015). Transgender affirmative cognitive behavioral therapy: Clinical considerations and applications. *Professional Psychology: Research and Practice, 46*(1), 21-29.

Bao, A.-M. & Swaab, D. F. (2011). Sexual differentiation of the human brain: Relation to gender identity, sexual orientation and neuropsychiatric disorders. *Frontiers in Neuroendocrinology, 32*(2), 214-226.

Baril, A. & Trevenen, K. (2014). Exploring ableism and cisnormativity in the conceptualization of identity and sexuality "disorders". *Annual Review of Critical Psychology, 11*(1), 389-416.

Baron-Cohen, S. (2004). *The essential difference*. London, New York: Penguin Books.

Benjamin, H. (1954). Transsexualism and Transvestism as Psychosomatic and Somatopsychic Syndromes. *American Journal of Psychotherapy, 8*(2), 219-230.

Benjamin, H. (1966). *The Transsexual Phenomenon*. New York: The Julian Press.

Benjamin, H. (1967). Transvestism and transsexualism. *JAMA, 199*(2), 136.

Benjamin, H. & Ihlenfeld, C. L. (1973). Transsexualism. *The American Journal of Nursing, 73*(3), 457-461.

Bergman, R.T., Howard, A.H. & Barnes, R.W. (1948). Plastic Reconstruction of the Penis. *The Journal of Urology, 59*(6), 1174-1182.

Bess, J. & Stabb, S. (2009). The experiences of transgendered persons in psychotherapy: Voices and recommendations. *Journal of Mental Health Counseling, 31*(3), 264-282.

Bleasdale, B., Finnegan, S., Murray, K., Kelly, S. & Percival, S. L. (2015). The use of silicone adhesives for scar reduction. *Advances in wound care, 4*(7), 422-430.

Bloch, M., Daly, R.C. & Rubinow, D. R. (2003). Endocrine factors in the etiology of postpartum depression. *Comprehensive psychiatry, 44*(3), 234-246.

Bouman, M.-B. (2016). *Total laparoscopic sigmoid vaginoplasty: A novel technique for primary and revision vaginoplasty.* (PhD thesis), Vrije Universiteit, Amsterdam.

Bouman, M.-B., Buncamper, M. E., van der Sluis, W. B. & Meijerink, W. J. (2016). Total laparoscopic sigmoid vaginoplasty. *Fertility and sterility, 106*(7), e22-e23.

Brighouse, D. (2001). Hormone replacement therapy (HRT) and anaesthesia. *BJA: British Journal of Anaesthesia, 86*(5), 709-716.

Brill, S. & Pepper, R. (2008). *The transgender child: A handbook for families and professionals.* San Francisco: Cleis Press.

British Psychoanalytic Council. (2017). UK organisations unite against Conversion Therapy Retrieved from https://www.bpc.org.uk/news/uk-organisations-unite-against-conversion-therapy-solidarity-minded-organisations-usa

Brown, G. R. & Jones, K. T. (2015). Incidence of breast cancer in a cohort of 5,135 transgender veterans. *Breast Cancer Research and Treatment, 149*(1), 191-198.

Bullough, V. L. & Bullough, B. (1993). *Cross dressing, sex, and gender.* Philadelphia: University of Pennsylvania Press.

Butler, G. (2017). Hormone Treatment for Transgender Children and Adolescents: Puberty, Blockers, Sex-Hormones and Helping Me Fit My True Gender Identity. In W. P. Bouman & J. Arcelus (Eds.), *The Transgender Handbook* (pp. 217-226). New York: Nova Science Publishers.

Butler, J. (1990). *Gender Trouble: Feminism and the Subversion of Identity.* London, New York: Routledge.

Butler, J. (1993). *Bodies That Matter: On the discursive limits of "sex".* London, New York: Routledge.

Capitán, L., Simon, D., Kaye, K. & Tenorio, T. (2014). Facial feminization surgery: The forehead. Surgical techniques and analysis of results. *Plastic and reconstructive surgery, 134*(4), 609-619.

Capitán, L., Simon, D., Meyer, T., Alcaide, A., Wells, A., Bailón, C. & Capitán-Cañadas, F. (2017). Facial feminization surgery: Simultaneous hair transplant during forehead reconstruction. *Plastic and reconstructive surgery, 139*(3), 573-584.

Cauldwell, D. (1949). Psychopathia Transsexualis. *Sexology, 16*, 274-280.

Chang, T.-S. & Hwang, W.-Y. (1984). Forearm flap in one-stage reconstruction of the penis. *Plastic and reconstructive surgery, 74*(2), 251-258.

Chang, T.K. & Chung, Y. B. (2015). Transgender Microaggressions: Complexity of the Heterogeneity of Transgender Identities. *Journal of LGBT Issues in Counseling, 9*(3), 217-234.

Chen, W., Mempel, M., Schober, W., Behrendt, H. & Ring, J. (2008). Gender difference, sex hormones, and immediate type hypersensitivity reactions. *Allergy, 63*(11), 1418-1427.

Cho, D. Y., Massie, J. P. & Morrison, S. D. (2017). Ethnic Considerations for Rhinoplasty in Facial Feminization. *JAMA facial plastic surgery, 19*(3), 243-243.

Cho, S.-W. & Jin, H.R. (2012). Feminization of the forehead in a transgender: Frontal sinus reshaping combined with brow lift and hairline lowering. *Aesthetic plastic surgery, 36*(5), 1207-1210.

Choi, I.S. (2011). Gender-specific asthma treatment. *Allergy, asthma & immunology research, 3*(2), 74-80.

Christopher, N., Ralph, D. & Garaffa, G. (2017). Genital Reconstructive Surgery for Transgender Men. In W.P. Bouman & J. Arcelus (Eds.), *The Transgender Handbook* (pp. 277-300). New York: Nova Science Publishers.

Cicero, E.C. & Black, B.P. (2016). "I Was a Spectacle... A Freak Show at the Circus": A Transgender Person's ED Experience and Implications for Nursing Practice. *Journal of Emergency Nursing, 42*(1), 25-30.

Clements-Nolle, K., Marx, R. & Katz, M. (2006). Attempted suicide among transgender persons: The influence of gender-based discrimination and victimization. *Journal of Homosexuality, 51*(3), 53-69.

Cohen, L., deRuiter, C., Ringelberg, H. & Cohen-Kettenis, P. (1997). Psychological functioning of adolescent transsexuals: Personality and psychopathology. *Journal of Clinical Psychology, 53*(2), 187-196.

Colapinto, J. (2000). *As nature made him: The boy who was raised as a girl.* New York: Harper Collins Publishers.

Cole, C. M., O'boyle, M., Emory, L. E. & Meyer III, W. J. (1997). Comorbidity of gender dysphoria and other major psychiatric diagnoses. *Archives of Sexual Behavior, 26*(1), 13-26.

Cole, E. (2015). Honest, open and non-judgemental: The cliniQ service is offering trans and non-binary people health care with dignity, writes Elaine Cole. *Nursing Standard, 29*(23), 19-21.

Coleman, E., Bockting, W., Botzer, M., Cohen-Kettenis, P., DeCuypere, G., Feldman, J. & Meyer, W. J. (2012). Standards of care for the health of transsexual, transgender, and gender-nonconforming people, version 7. *International Journal of Transgenderism, 13*(4), 165-232.

Cook, M. B., Dawsey, S. M., Freedman, N. D., Inskip, P. D., Wichner, S.M., Quraishi, S. M. & McGlynn, K. A. (2009). Sex disparities in cancer incidence by period and age. *Cancer Epidemiology and Prevention Biomarkers, 18*(4), 1174-1182.

Creighton, S., Alderson, J., Brown, S. & Minto, C. (2002). Medical photography: ethics, consent and the intersex patient. *BJU international, 89*(1), 67-71.

Cromwell, J. (1999). Passing women and female-bodied men: (Re)claiming FTM history. In S. Whittle & K. More (Eds.), *Reclaiming Genders: Transsexual Grammars at the Fin de Siecle* (pp. 34-61). London and New York: Cassell.

Da Silva, J.A.P. (1999). Sex hormones and glucocorticoids: interactions with the immune system. *Annals of the New York Academy of Sciences, 876*(1), 102-118.

Davidge-Pitts, C., Nippoldt, T. B., Danoff, A., Radziejewski, L. & Natt, N. (2017). Transgender health in endocrinology: Current status of endocrinology fellowship programs and practicing clinicians. *The Journal of Clinical Endocrinology & Metabolism, 102*(4), 1286-1290.

De Roo, C., Tilleman, K., T'Sjoen, G. & De Sutter, P. (2016). Fertility options in transgender people. *International Review of Psychiatry, 28*(1), 112-119.

Delemarre-van de Waal, H. A. & Cohen-Kettenis, P. T. (2006). Clinical management of gender identity disorder in adolescents: a protocol on psychological and paediatric endocrinology aspects. *European journal of endocrinology, 155*(suppl 1), S131-S137.

Descamps, M., Hayes, P. & Hudson, D. A. (2009). Phalloplasty in complete aphallia: pedicled anterolateral thigh flap. *Journal of Plastic, Reconstructive & Aesthetic Surgery, 62*(3), e51-e54.

Deutsch, M.B. (2016). Guidelines for the Primary and Gender-Affirming Care of Transgender and Gender Nonbinary People. Retrieved from http://transhealth.ucsf.edu/pdf/Transgender-PGACG-6-17-16.pdf

Deutsch, M.B. (2017). Overview of feminizing hormone therapy. Retrieved from http://transhealth.ucsf.edu/trans?page=guidelines-feminizing-therapy

Dhand, A. & Dhaliwal, G. (2010). Examining patient conceptions: a case of metastatic breast cancer in an African American male to female transgender patient. *Journal of General Internal Medicine, 25*(2), 158-161.

Dhejne, C., Öberg, K., Arver, S. & Landén, M. (2014). An analysis of all applications for sex reassignment surgery in Sweden, 1960–2010: prevalence, incidence, and regrets. *Archives of Sexual Behavior, 43*(8), 1535-1545.

Di Ceglie, D., Freedman, D., McPherson, S. & Richardson, P. (2002). Children and Adolescents Referred to a Specialist Gender Identity Development Service: Clinical Features and Demographic Characteristics. *International Journal of Transgenderism, 6*(1), no pagination.

Diamond, M. & Sigmundson, H. K. (1997). Sex reassignment at birth: Long-term review and clinical implications. *Archives of pediatrics & adolescent medicine, 151*(3), 298-304.

Dillon, M. (1946) *Self: A study in endocrinology and ethics.* London: William Heinemann.

Djordjevic, M., Bizic, M., Stanojevic, D., Bumbasirevic, M., Kojovic, V., Majstorovic, M. & Perovic, S. (2009). Urethral lengthening in metoidioplasty (female-to-male sex reassignment surgery) by combined buccal mucosa graft and labia minora flap. *Urology, 74*(2), 349-353.

Djordjevic, M. L. & Bizic, M. R. (2013). Comparison of two different methods for urethral lengthening in female to male (metoidioplasty) surgery. *The Journal of Sexual Medicine, 10*(5), 1431-1438.

Donovan, T. (2001). Being transgender and older: A first person account. *Journal of Gay & Lesbian Social Services, 13*(4), 19-22.

Dorak, M. T. & Karpuzoglu, E. (2012). Gender differences in cancer susceptibility: an inadequately addressed issue. *Frontiers in genetics, 3*, 268.

Drescher, J., Cohen-Kettenis, P. & Winter, S. (2012). Minding the body: Situating gender identity diagnoses in the ICD-11. *International Review of Psychiatry, 24*(6), 568-577.

Drummond, K. D., Bradley, S. J., Peterson-Badali, M. & Zucker, K. J. (2008). A follow-up study of girls with gender identity disorder. *Developmental psychology, 44*(1), 34-45.

Duckett, J. W. & Baskin, L. S. (1993). Genitoplasty for intersex anomalies. *European Journal of Pediatrics, 152*(Suppl. 2), 580-584.

DunnGalvin, A., Hourihane, J. B., Frewer, L., Knibb, R., Oude Elberink, J. & Klinge, I. (2006). Incorporating a gender dimension in food allergy research: a review. *Allergy, 61*(11), 1336-1343.

Durand, C., Alhammad, A. & Willett, K. C. (2012). Practical considerations for optimal transdermal drug delivery. *American Journal of Health-System Pharmacy, 69*(2), 116-124.

Dutton, L., Koenig, K. & Fennie, K. (2008). Gynecologic care of the female-to-male transgender man. *Journal of Midwifery & Women's Health, 53*(4), 331-337.

Ehrensaft, D. (2016). *The Gender Creative Child: Pathways for Nurturing and Supporting Children Who Live Outside Gender Boxes.* New York: The Experiment.

Ellis, H. (1927). *Studies in the Psychology of Sex Volume II: Sexual Inversion* (3rd ed.). Philadelphia: F. A. Davis Co.

Ellis, S. J., Bailey, L. & McNeil, J. (2015). Trans people's experiences of mental health and gender identity services: A UK study. *Journal of Gay & Lesbian Mental Health, 19*(1), 4-20.

Ellsworth, W. A. & Colon, G. A. (2006). Management of medical morbidities and risk factors before surgery: smoking, diabetes, and other complicating factors. *Seminars in Plastic Surgery, 20*(4), 205-213.

Equality Act. (2010). *chapter 1, section 7.* London: The Stationery Office Retrieved from http://www.legislation.gov.uk/ukpga/2010/15/section/7.

Erickson-Schroth, L. & Jacobs, L. A. (2017). *"You're in the Wrong Bathroom!": And 20 Other Myths and Misconceptions About Transgender and Gender-Nonconforming People.* Boston: Beacon Press.

Ezie, C. (2011). Deconstructing the Body: Transgender and Intersex Identities and Sex Discrimination-The Need for Strict Scrutiny. *Columbia Journal of Gender and Law, 20*(1), 141-199.

Fausto-Sterling, A. (1993). The five sexes. *The sciences, 33*(2), 20-24.

Fausto-Sterling, A. (2000). The five sexes, revisited. *The Sciences, 40*(4), 18-23.

Fausto-Sterling, A. (2008). *Myths of gender: Biological theories about women and men* (2nd ed.). New York: Basic Books.

Feldman, J., Brown, G. R., Deutsch, M. B., Hembree, W., Meyer, W., Meyer-Bahlburg, H. F. & Safer, J. D. (2016). Priorities for transgender medical and healthcare research. *Current Opinion in Endocrinology, Diabetes and Obesity, 23*(2), 180-187.

Fine, C. (2010). *Delusions of gender.* London: Icon.

Fletcher, D. E. (1991). The eternal battle of sex vs gender. *JAMA, 266*(20), 2833.

Freidenberg, C. B. (2002). Working with male-to-female transgendered clients: Clinical considerations. *Contemporary Issues in Communication Science and Disorders, 29*(1), 43-58.

Frey, J. D., Poudrier, G., Chiodo, M. V. & Hazen, A. (2017). Research disparities in female-to-male transgender genital reconstruction: the charge for high-quality data on patient reported outcome measures. *Annals of Plastic Surgery, 78*(3), 241.

Gallieni, M., Mezzina, N., Pinerolo, C. & Granata, A. (2012). Sex and gender differences in nephrology. In S. Oertelt-Prigione & V. Regitz-Zagrosek (Eds.), *Sex and gender aspects in clinical medicine* (pp. 83-100). London, Dordrecht, Heidelberg, New York: Springer.

Gamarel, K. E., Reisner, S. L., Laurenceau, J.-P., Nemoto, T. & Operario, D. (2014). Gender minority stress, mental health, and relationship quality: A dyadic investigation of transgender women and their cisgender male partners. *Journal of Family Psychology, 28*(4), 437-447.

Garfinkel, H. (2006). Passing and the Managed Achievement of Sex Status in an Intersexed Person, Part 1. In Susan Stryker & S. Whittle (Eds.), *The transgender studies reader* (pp. 58-93). New York and London: Routledge.

Garrett, N. R. (2004). Treatment of a transgender client with schizophrenia in a public psychiatric milieu: A case study by a student therapist. *Journal of Gay & Lesbian Psychotherapy, 8*(3-4), 127-141.

Gearhart, J. P. & Rock, J. (1989). Total ablation of the penis after circumcision with electrocautery: a method of management and long-term followup. *The Journal of urology, 142*(3), 799-801.

Giltay, E. J. & Gooren, L. J. (2000). Effects of sex steroid deprivation/administration on hair growth and skin sebum production in transsexual males and females. *Journal of Clinical Endocrinology and Metabolism, 85*(8), 2913-2921.

Ginsberg, B. (2016). Dermatologic care of the transgender patient. *International JOurnal of Women's Dermatology, 3*(1), 65-67.

Gomes de Jesus, J. (2014). Gender without Essentialism: Transgender Feminism as a Critique of Sex. *Universitas Humanística, 78,* 241-257. Retrieved from http://www.scielo.org.co/scielo.php?script=sci_arttext&pid=S0120-48072014000200011&lng=en&nrm=iso

Gooren, L. J., Giltay, E. J. & Bunck, M. C. (2008). Long-term treatment of transsexuals with cross-sex hormones: extensive personal experience. *The Journal of Clinical Endocrinology & Metabolism, 93*(1), 19-25.

Gooren, L. J., Trotsenburg, M. A., Giltay, E. J. & Diest, P. J. (2013). Breast cancer development in transsexual subjects receiving cross-sex hormone treatment. *The Journal of Sexual Medicine, 10*(12), 3129-3134.

Grant, J. M., Mottet, L., Tanis, J. E., Harrison, J., Herman, J. & Keisling, M. (2011). Injustice at every turn: A report of the National Transgender Discrimination Survey. Retrieved from http://www.thetaskforce.org/static_html/downloads/reports/reports/ntds_full.pdf

Greener, H. (2014). Guidelines for the use of feminising hormone therapy in gender dysphoria. Retrieved from http://www.northoftyneapc.nhs.uk/wp-content/uploads/sites/6/2017/04/Gender-Dysphoria-Feminising-Hormones-Mar-2017.pdf

Greenspan, J. D., Craft, R. M., LeResche, L., Arendt-Nielsen, L., Berkley, K. J., Fillingim, R. B. & Mayer, E. A. (2007). Studying sex and gender differences in pain and analgesia: a consensus report. *Pain, 132*(Nov.), S26-S45.

Greytak, E. A., Kosciw, J. G. & Boesen, M. J. (2013). Putting the "T" in "resource": The benefits of LGBT-related school resources for transgender youth. *Journal of LGBT Youth, 10*(1-2), 45-63.

Grossman, A. H. & D'Augelli, A. R. (2007). Transgender Youth and Life-Threatening Behaviours. *Suicide and Life-Threatening Behavior, 37*(5), 527-537.

Haas, A. P., Rodgers, P. L. & Herman, J. L. (2014). Suicide attempts among transgender and gender non-conforming adults. Retrieved from https://queeramnesty.ch/docs/AFSP-Williams-Suicide-Report-Final.pdf

Haedersdal, M. & Wulf, H. (2006). Evidence-based review of hair removal using lasers and light sources. *Journal of the European Academy of Dermatology and Venereology, 20*(1), 9-20.

Hage, J., Dekker, J., Karim, R., Verheijen, R. & Bloemena, E. (2000). Ovarian cancer in female-to-male transsexuals: report of two cases. *Gynecologic oncology, 76*(3), 413-415.

Hage, J. J. & Karim, R. B. (1998). Abdominoplastic secondary full-thickness skin graft vaginoplasty for male-to-female transsexuals. *Plastic and reconstructive surgery, 101*(6), 1512-1515.

Harris, M., Kondel, L. & Dorsen, C. (2017). Pelvic pain in transgender men taking testosterone: Assessing the risk of ovarian cancer. *The Nurse Practitioner, 42*(7), 1-5.

Hashmi, A., Hanif, F., Hanif, S. M., Abdullah, F. E. & Shamim, M. S. (2008). Complete androgen insensitivity syndrome. *J Coll Physicians Surg Pak, 18*(7), 442-444.

Heck, N. C., Flentje, A. & Cochran, B. N. (2011). Offsetting risks: High school gay-straight alliances and lesbian, gay, bisexual, and transgender (LGBT) youth. *School Psychology Quarterly, 26*(2), 161-174.

Hembree, W. C. (2011). Guidelines for pubertal suspension and gender reassignment for transgender adolescents. *Child and Adolescent Psychiatric Clinics, 20*(4), 725-732.

Hembree, W. C., Cohen-Kettenis, P., Delemarre-Van De Waal, H. A., Gooren, L. J., Meyer III, W. J., Spack, N. P. & Montori, V. M. (2009). Endocrine treatment of transsexual persons: an Endocrine Society clinical practice guideline. *The Journal of Clinical Endocrinology & Metabolism, 94*(9), 3132-3154.

Hendricks, M. L. & Testa, R. J. (2012). A conceptual framework for clinical work with transgender and gender nonconforming clients: An adaptation of the Minority Stress Model. *Professional Psychology-Research and Practice, 43*(5), 460-467.

Herdt, G. H. (1993). *Third Sex, Third Gender: Beyond Sexual Dimorphism in Culture and History*. New York: Zone Books.

Hirschfeld, M. (1910). *Die Transvestiten: eine Untersuchung über den erotischen Verkleidungstrieb: mit umfangreichen casuistischen und historischen Material*. Berlin: A. Pulvermacher.

Hirschfeld, M. (1923). Die intersexuelle konstitution. *Jahrbuch für sexuelle Zwischenstufen, 23*, 3-27.

Horbach, S. E., Bouman, M. B., Smit, J. M., Özer, M., Buncamper, M. E. & Mullender, M. G. (2015). Outcome of Vaginoplasty in Male-to-Female Transgenders: A Systematic Review of Surgical Techniques. *The Journal of Sexual Medicine, 12*(6), 1499-1512.

Hoshiai, M., Matsumoto, Y., Sato, T., Ohnishi, M., Okabe, N., Kishimoto, Y. & Kuroda, S. (2010). Psychiatric comorbidity among patients with gender identity disorder. *Psychiatry and Clinical Neurosciences, 64*(5), 514-519.

Hoymork, S. & Raeder, J. (2005). Why do women wake up faster than men from propofol anaesthesia? *British journal of anaesthesia, 95*(5), 627-633.

Huddleston, R. & Pullum, G. K. (2002). *The Cambridge Grammar of English Language*. Cambridge: Cambridge University Press.

Iverson, C. (1991). The Eternal Battle of Sex vs Gender-Reply. *JAMA, 266*(20), 2833.

James, A. (2017). Electrolysis. Retrieved from http://www.tsroadmap.com/physical/hair/zapidx.html

James, J. (2013). *Transgender Health Care*. (Doctor of Nursing Practice), St. Catherine University, Retrieved from https://sophia.stkate.edu/cgi/viewcontent.cgi?article=1041&context=dnp_projects

Jarrold, C. & Brock, J. (2004). To match or not to match? Methodological issues in autism-related research. *Journal of autism and developmental disorders, 34*(1), 81-86.

Kandhro, A. (2016). Hematological parameters in Transgender Persons. *Hematology and Transfusion International Journal, 2*(4), 1-2.

Katz, J. (2007). *The Invention of Heterosexuality*. Chicago: University of Chicago Press.

Kelleher, C. (2009). Minority stress and health: Implications for lesbian, gay, bisexual, transgender, and questioning (LGBTQ) young people. *Counselling Psychology Quarterly, 22*(4), 373-379.

Kessler, S. J. & McKenna, W. (1978). *Gender: An Ethnomethodological Approach*. Chicago, London: University of Chicago Press.

Klein, A., Steinert, S., Baeumler, W., Landthaler, M. & Babilas, P. (2013). Photoepilation with a diode laser vs. intense pulsed light: a randomized, intrapatient left-to-right trial. *British Journal of Dermatology, 168*(6), 1287-1293.

Kolvenbag, G. J. & Blackledge, G. R. (1996). Worldwide activity and safety of bicalutamide: a summary review. *Urology, 47*(1), 70-79.

Kreukels, B. P., Steensma, T. D. & De Vries, A. L. (Eds.). (2014). *Gender Dysphoria and Disorders of Sex Development: Progress in Care and Knowledge*. New York, Heidelberg, Dordrecht, London: Springer.

Laqueur, T. W. (1990). *Making sex: Body and gender from the Greeks to Freud*. Harvard: Harvard University Press.

Lawrence, A. A. (2003). Factors associated with satisfaction or regret following male-to-female sex reassignment surgery. *Archives of Sexual Behavior, 32*(4), 299-315.

Lester, C. (2017). *trans like me: a journey for all of us*. London: Virago Press.

Levesque, P. (2015). Meeting the Needs of the Transgender Nursing Student. *Nurse educator, 40*(5), 244-248.

Light, A. D., Obedin-Maliver, J., Sevelius, J. M. & Kerns, J. L. (2014). Transgender men who experienced pregnancy after female-to-male gender transitioning. *Obstetrics & Gynecology, 124*(6), 1120-1127.

Logie, C., Bridge, T. J. & Bridge, P. D. (2007). Evaluating the phobias, attitudes, and cultural competence of master of social work students toward the LGBT populations. *Journal of Homosexuality, 53*(4), 201-221.

Luecke, J. C. (2011). Working with Transgender Children and Their Classmares in Pre-Adolescence: Just Be Supportive. *Journal of LGBT Youth, 8*(2), 116-156.

MacNamara, J., Glann, S. & Durlak, P. (2017). Experiencing Misgendered Pronouns: A Classroom Activity to Encourage Empathy. *Teaching Sociology, 45*(3), 269-278.

Maguen, S., Shipherd, J. C. & Harris, H. N. (2005). Providing culturally sensitive care for transgender patients. *Cognitive and Behavioral Practice, 12*(4), 479-490.

Manders, E. K., Graham III, W. P., Schenden, M. J. & Davis, T. S. (1984). Skin expansion to eliminate large scalp defects. *Annals of plastic surgery, 12*(4), 305-312.

Manson, J. E., Hsia, J., Johnson, K. C., Rossouw, J. E., Assaf, A. R., Lasser, N. L., . . . Detrano, R. (2003). Estrogen plus progestin and the risk of coronary heart disease. *New England Journal of Medicine, 349*(6), 523-534.

Mastronikolis, N. S., Remacle, M., Biagini, M., Kiagiadaki, D. & Lawson, G. (2013). Wendler glottoplasty: an effective pitch raising surgery in male-to-female transsexuals. *Journal of Voice, 27*(4), 516-522.

Mayer, E. A., Berman, S., Chang, L. & Naliboff, B. D. (2004). Sex-based differences in gastrointestinal pain. *European Journal of Pain, 8*(5), 451-463.

Mayer, T. G. & Fleming, R. W. (1985). Hairline aesthetics and styling in hair replacement surgery. *Head & Neck, 7*(4), 286-302.

McDowell, A. & Bower, K. M. (2016). Transgender health care for nurses: An innovative approach to diversifying nursing curricula to address health inequities. *Journal of Nursing Education, 55*(8), 476-479.

McLemore, K. A. (2015). Experiences with misgendering: Identity misclassification of transgender spectrum individuals. *Self and Identity, 14*(1), 51-74.

McNeil, J., Bailey, L., Ellis, S., Morton, J. & Regan, M. (2012). Trans Mental Health Study 2012. Retrieved from http://worldaa1.miniserver.com/~gires/assets/Medpro-Assets/trans_mh_study.pdf

Meyer, I. H. (2003). Prejudice, social stress, and mental health in lesbian, gay, and bisexual populations: conceptual issues and research evidence. *Psychological bulletin, 129*(5), 674-697.

Miksad, R. A., Bubley, G., Church, P., Sanda, M., Rofsky, N., Kaplan, I. & Cooper, A. (2006). Prostate cancer in a transgender woman 41 years after initiation of feminization. *JAMA, 296*(19), 2312-2317.

Mills, M. & Stoneham, G. (2017). *The Voice Book for Trans and Non-Binary People*. London and Philadelphia: Jessica Kingsley Publishers.

Mitu, K. (2016). Transgender Reproductive Choice and Fertility Preservation. *AMA journal of ethics, 18*(11), 1119-1125.

Money, J. (1986). *Lovemaps: Clinical concepts of sexual/erotic health and pathology, paraphilia, and gender transposition of childhood, adolescence, and maturity*. New York: Irvington Publishers.

Money, J. & Ehrhardt, A. A. (1972). *Man and woman, boy and girl: Differentiation and dimorphism of gender identity from conception to maturity*. Oxford: John Hopkins University Press.

Money, J., Hampson, J. G. & Hampson, J. L. (1955). An examination of some basic sexual concepts: the evidence of human hermaphroditism. *Bulletin of the Johns Hopkins Hospital, 97*(4), 301-319.

Morrison, S. D., Vyas, K. S., Motakef, S., Gast, K. M., Chung, M. T., Rashidi, V. & Cederna, P. S. (2016). Facial feminization: systematic review of the literature. *Plastic and reconstructive surgery, 137*(6), 1759-1770.

Moser, C. & Kleinplatz, P. J. (2006). DSM-IV-TR and the paraphilias: An argument for removal. *Journal of Psychology & Human Sexuality, 17*(3-4), 91-109.

Murphy, S., Khaw, K.-T., Sneyd, M. J. & Compston, J. E. (1992). Endogenous sex hormones and bone mineral density among community-based postmenopausal women. *Postgraduate medical journal, 68*(805), 908-913.

Murphy, T. F. (2015). Assisted gestation and transgender women. *Bioethics, 29*(6), 389-397.

Nadal, K. L., Davidoff, K. C. & Fujii-Doe, W. (2014). Transgender women and the sex work industry: Roots in systemic, institutional, and interpersonal discrimination. *Journal of Trauma & Dissociation, 15*(2), 169-183.

Naugler, W. E., Sakurai, T., Kim, S., Maeda, S., Kim, K., Elsharkawy, A. M. & Karin, M. (2007). Gender disparity in liver cancer due to sex differences in MyD88-dependent IL-6 production. *Science, 317*(5834), 121-124.

Nelson, L., Whallett, E. & McGregor, J. (2009). Transgender patient satisfaction following reduction mammaplasty. *Journal of Plastic, Reconstructive & Aesthetic Surgery, 62*(3), 331-334.

Nelles, J. L., Hu, W. Y. & Prins, G. S. (2011). Estrogen action and prostate cancer. *Expert review of endocrinology & metabolism, 6*(3), 437-451.

Newhook, J.T., Pyne, J., Winters, K., Feder, S., Holmes, C., Tosh, J., and Pickett, S. (2018) A critical commentary on follow-up studies and "desistance" theories about transgender and gender-nonconforming children. *International Journal of Transgenderism*. DOI: 10.1080/15532739.2018.1456390

NHS England. (2007). A guide to hormone therapy for trans people. Retrieved from http://www.teni.ie/attachments/9ea50d6e-1148-4c26-be0d-9def980047db.PDF

NHS England. (2013). *Interim NHS England Gender Dysphoria Protocol and Service Guideline 2013/14*. London: NHS England Retrieved from https://www.england.nhs.uk/wp-content/uploads/2013/10/int-gend-proto.pdf.

NHS England, NHS Scotland, The Scottish Government, Association of Christian Counsellors, British Association for Behavioural and Cognitive Psychotherapies, British Association for Counselling and Psychotherapy & UK Council for Psychotherapy. (2015). Memorandum of Understanding on Conversion Therapy in the UK. Retrieved from https://www.psychotherapy.org.uk/wp-content/uploads/2016/09/Memorandum-of-understanding-on-conversion-therapy.pdf

Nicolai, T., Pereszlenyiova-Bliznakova, L., Illi, S., Reinhardt, D. & Von Mutius, E. (2003). Longitudinal follow-up of the changing gender ratio in asthma from childhood to adulthood: role of delayed manifestation in girls. *Pediatric allergy and immunology, 14*(4), 280-283.

Nikolic, D. V., Djordjevic, M. L., Granic, M., Nikolic, A. T., Stanimirovic, V. V., Zdravkovic, D. & Jelic, S. (2012). Importance of revealing a rare case of breast cancer in a female to male transsexual after bilateral mastectomy. *World Journal of Surgical Oncology, 10*(280), 1-4.

Obedin-Maliver, J. (2015). Time for OBGYNs to care for people of all genders. *Journal of Women's Health, 24*(2), 109-111.

Obedin-Maliver, J., Light, A., DeHaan, G., Steinauer, J. & Jackson, R. (2014). Vaginal Hysterectomy as a Viable Option for Female-to-Male Transgender Men. *Obstetrics & Gynecology, 123*, 126S-127S.

Oertelt-Prigione, S. & Regitz-Zagrosek, V. (2011). *Sex and gender aspects in clinical medicine.* London, Dordrecht, Heidelberg, New York: Springer.

Olsen, E. A. (1999). Methods of hair removal. *Journal of the American Academy of Dermatology, 40*(2), 143-155.

Olson, K. R., Durwood, L., DeMeules, M. & McLaughlin, K. A. (2016). Mental health of transgender children who are supported in their identities. *Pediatrics, 137*(3), 1-10.

Olsson, S.-E. & Möller, A. (2006). Regret after sex reassignment surgery in a male-to-female transsexual: A long-term follow-up. *Archives of Sexual Behavior, 35*(4), 501-506.

Operario, D., Soma, T. & Underhill, K. (2008). Sex work and HIV status among transgender women: systematic review and meta-analysis. *JAIDS Journal of Acquired Immune Deficiency Syndromes, 48*(1), 97-103.

Orloff, L. A., Mann, A. P., Damrose, J. F. & Goldman, S. N. (2006). Laser-Assisted Voice Adjustment (LAVA) in Transsexuals. *The Laryngoscope, 116*(4), 655-660.

Osman, M. (2003). Therapeutic implications of sex differences in asthma and atopy. *Archives of disease in childhood, 88*(7), 587-590.

Pauly, I. B. (1965). Male psychosexual inversion: Transsexualism: A review of 100 cases. *Archives of General Psychiatry, 13*(2), 172-181.

Peitzmeier, S., Gardner, I., Weinand, J., Corbet, A. & Acevedo, K. (2017). Health impact of chest binding among transgender adults: a community-engaged, cross-sectional study. *Culture, health & sexuality, 19*(1), 64-75.

Perlmutter, A. & Reitelman, C. (1992). Surgical management of intersexuality. In P. Walsh (Ed.), *Campbell's Urology* (Vol. 4, pp. 1951-1966). Philadelphia: WB Saunders.

Perovic, S., Stanojevic, D. & Djordjevic, M. (2000). Vaginoplasty in male transsexuals using penile skin and a urethral flap. *BJU international, 86*(7), 843-850.

Persson, D. I. (2009). Unique challenges of transgender aging: Implications from the literature. *Journal of Gerontological Social Work, 52*(6), 633-646.

Peters, P. (2004). *The Cambridge guide to English usage.* Cambridge: Cambridge University Press.

Pfafflin, F. (1993). Regrets after sex reassignment surgery. *Journal of Psychology & Human Sexuality, 5*(4), 69-85.

Phillips, J., Fein-Zachary, V. J., Mehta, T. S., Littlehale, N., Venkataraman, S. & Slanetz, P. J. (2014). Breast imaging in the transgender patient. *American Journal of Roentgenology, 202*(5), 1149-1156.

Pleym, H., Spigset, O., Kharasch, E. & Dale, O. (2003). Gender differences in drug effects: implications for anesthesiologists. *Acta anaesthesiologica scandinavica, 47*(3), 241-259.

Porter, K. E., Brennan-Ing, M., Chang, S. C., Dickey, L. M., Singh, A. A., Bower, K. L. & Witten, T. M. (2016). Providing competent and affirming services for transgender and gender nonconforming older adults. *Clinical Gerontologist, 39*(5), 366-388.

Prince, V. (1979). The life and times of Virginia. *Transvestia, 17*(100), 5-120.

Public Health England. (2017). Information for trans people. Retrieved from https://www.gov.uk/government/publications/nhs-population-screening-for-transgender-people

Rachlin, K., Hansbury, G. & Pardo, S. T. (2010). Hysterectomy and oophorectomy experiences of female-to-male transgender individuals. *International Journal of Transgenderism, 12*(3), 155-166.

Raphael, P., Harris, R. & Harris, S. W. (2014). The endonasal lip lift: personal technique. *Aesthetic surgery journal, 34*(3), 457-468.

Regitz-Zagrosek, V. (2012). Sex and gender differences in health. *EMBO reports, 13*(7), 596-603.

Reisner, S. L., Vetters, R., Leclerc, M., Zaslow, S., Wolfrum, S., Shumer, D. & Mimiaga, M. J. (2015). Mental health of transgender youth in care at an adolescent urban community health center: A matched retrospective cohort study. *Journal of Adolescent Health, 56*(3), 1-16.

Richards, C., Arcelus, J., Barrett, J., Bouman, W. P., Lenihan, P., Lorimer, S., . . . Seal, L. (2015). Trans is not a disorder–but should still receive funding. *Sexual and Relationship Therapy, 30*(3), 309-313.

Richards, C., Bouman, W. P. & Barker, M.-J. (Eds.). (2017). *Genderqueer and Non-Binary Genders.* London: Palgrave Macmillan.

Richards, C., Bouman, W. P., Seal, L., Barker, M. J., Nieder, T. O. & T'Sjoen, G. (2016). Non-binary or genderqueer genders. *International Review of Psychiatry, 28*(1), 1-8.

Richards, C. & Seal, L. (2014). Trans people's reproductive options and outcomes. *Journal of Family Planning and Reproductive Health Care, 0*, 1-3.

Richardson, N. (2016). *Transgressive bodies: Representations in film and popular culture*. London, New York: Routledge.

Rieder, E. A., Nagler, A. R. & Leger, M. C. (2016). In response to Ginsberg et al: "A potential role for the dermatologist in the physical transformation of transgender people: A survey of attitudes and practices within the transgender community". *Journal of the American Academy of Dermatology, 75*(2), e73.

Rohrich, R. J. & Bolden, K. (2010). Ethnic rhinoplasty. *Clinics in plastic surgery, 37*(2), 353-370.

Royal College of Obstetricians and Gynaecologists. (2017). FSRH CEU Statement: Contraceptive Choices and Sexual Health for Transgender and Non-binary People. Retrieved from https://www.fsrh.org/documents/fsrh-ceu-statement-contraceptive-choices-and-sexual-health-for/

Royal College of Psychatrists. (2014). Good practice guidelines for the assessment and treatment of adults with gender dysphoria *Sexual and Relationship Therapy, 29*(2), 154-214.

Rutegård, M., Shore, R., Lu, Y., Lagergren, P. & Lindblad, M. (2010). Sex differences in the incidence of gastrointestinal adenocarcinoma in Sweden 1970–2006. *European Journal of Cancer, 46*(6), 1093-1100.

Schmetzer, O. & Flörcken, A. (2011). Sex and Gender Differences in Hematology. In S. Oertelt-Prigione & V. Regitz-Zagrosek (Eds.), *Sex and gender aspects in clinical medicine* (pp. 151-168). London, Dordrecht, Heidelberg, New York: Springer.

Schmitt, S. (2013). Checking Our Privilege, Working Together: Notes on Virtual Trans* Communities, Truscum Blogs, and the Politics of Transgender Health Care. Retrieved from http://thefeministwire.com/2013/07/checking-our-privilege-working-together-notes-on-virtual-trans-communities-truscum-blogs-and-the-politics-of-transgender-health-care

Schultheiss, D., Gabouev, A. I. & Jonas, U. (2005). HISTORY: Nikolaj A. Bogoraz (1874–1952): Pioneer of Phalloplasty and Penile Implant Surgery. *The Journal of Sexual Medicine, 2*(1), 139-146.

Schuster, M. A., Reisner, S. L. & Onorato, S. E. (2016). Beyond bathrooms—meeting the health needs of transgender people. *New England Journal of Medicine, 375*(2), 101-103.

Seal, L., Franklin, S., Richards, C., Shishkareva, A., Sinclaire, C. & Barrett, J. (2012). Predictive markers for mammoplasty and a comparison of side effect profiles in transwomen taking various hormonal regimens. *The Journal of Clinical Endocrinology & Metabolism, 97*(12), 4422-4428.

Seal, L. J. (2007). The Hormonal Management of adults with gender dysphoria. In J. Barrett (Ed.), *Transexual and Other Disorders of Gender Identity: A practical guide to management* (pp. 157-185). London: Radcliffe Publishing.

Seelman, K. L. (2014). Transgender individuals' access to college housing and bathrooms: Findings from the National Transgender Discrimination Survey. *Journal of Gay & Lesbian Social Services, 26*(2), 186-206.

Selvaggi, G. & Andreasson, M. (2017). Genital Reconstructive Surgery for Transgender Women. In W. P. Bouman & J. Arcelus (Eds.), *The Transgender Handbook* (pp. 265-275). New York: Nova Science Publishers.

Selvaggi, G., Monstrey, S., Hoebeke, P., Ceulemans, P., Van Landuyt, K., Hamdi, M. & Blondeel, P. (2006). Donor-site morbidity of the radial forearm free flap after 125 phalloplasties in gender identity disorder. *Plastic and reconstructive surgery, 118*(5), 1171-1177.

Serano, J. (2007). *Whipping girl: A transsexual woman on sexism and the scapegoating of femininity*. Berkeley: Seal Press.

Shatzel, J. J., Connelly, K. J. & DeLoughery, T. G. (2017). Thrombotic issues in transgender medicine: a review. *American journal of hematology, 92*(2), 204-208.

Shiotani, A., Miyanishi, T. & Takahashi, T. (2006). Sex differences in irritable bowel syndrome in Japanese university students. *Journal of gastroenterology, 41*(6), 562-568.

Sigurjónsson, H., Möllermark, C., Rinder, J., Farnebo, F. & Lundgren, T. K. (2017). Long-term sensitivity and patient-reported functionality of the neoclitoris after gender reassignment surgery. *The Journal of Sexual Medicine, 14*(2), 269-273.

Silbiger, S. & Neugarten, J. (2008). Gender and human chronic renal disease. *Gender medicine, 5*, S3-S10.

Simons, L., Schrager, S. M., Clark, L. F., Belzer, M. & Olson, J. (2013). Parental Support and Mental Health Among Transgender Adolescents. *Journal of Adolescent Health, 53*(6), 1-7.

Siverskog, A. (2014). "They just don't have a clue": Transgender aging and implications for social work. *Journal of Gerontological Social Work, 57*(2-4), 386-406.

Snelgrove, J. W., Jasudavisius, A. M., Rowe, B. W., Head, E. M. & Bauer, G. R. (2012). "Completely out-at-sea" with "two-gender medicine": A qualitative analysis of physician-side barriers to providing healthcare for transgender patients. *BMC health services research, 12*(110), 1-13.

Spiegel, J. H. (2017). Rhinoplasty as a significant component of facial feminization and beautification. *JAMA facial plastic surgery, 19*(3), 181-182.

Steensma, T. D., Biemond, R., de Boer, F. & Cohen-Kettenis, P. T. (2011). Desisting and persisting gender dysphoria after childhood: A qualitative follow-up study. *Clinical child psychology and psychiatry, 16*(4), 499-516.

Steensma, T. D., McGuire, J. K., Kreukels, B. P., Beekman, A. J. & Cohen-Kettenis, P. T. (2013). Factors associated with desistence and persistence of childhood gender dysphoria: a quantitative follow-up study. *Journal of the American Academy of Child & Adolescent Psychiatry, 52*(6), 582-590.

Stonewall. (2017). School Report: The experiences of lesbian, gay, bi and trans young people in Britain's schools in 2017. Retrieved from https://www.stonewall.org.uk/sites/default/files/the_school_report_2017.pdf

Strandjord, S. E., Ng, H. & Rome, E. S. (2015). Effects of treating gender dysphoria and anorexia nervosa in a transgender adolescent: lessons learned. *International Journal of Eating Disorders, 48*(7), 942-945.

Streed, C. G., Harfouch, O., Marvel, F., Blumenthal, R. S., Martin, S. S. & Mukherjee, M. (2017). Cardiovascular Disease Among Transgender Adults Receiving Hormone TherapyA Narrative ReviewCardiovascular Disease Among Transgender Adults. *Annals of Internal Medicine, 167*(4), 256-267.

Stryker, S. (2008). *Transgender History*. Berkeley: Seal Press.

Sunderland Clinical Commisioning Group. (2014). Guidelines for the use of masculinising hormone therapy in gender dysphoria. Retrieved from http://sunderlandccg.nhs.uk/wp-content/uploads/2016/03/SCCG-Gender-Dysphoria-Masculinising-Hormones-Dec-2015.pdf?UNLID=44982169920179279483

T'Sjoen, G., Van Caenegem, E. & Wierckx, K. (2013). Transgenderism and reproduction. *Current Opinion in Endocrinology, Diabetes and Obesity, 20*(6), 575-579.

Thomas, T. N. & Unger, C. A. (2017). Vaginoplasty for the Transgender Woman. *Current Obstetrics and Gynecology Reports, 6*(2), 133-139.

Thompson, G. W. (1997). Gender differences in irritable bowel symptoms. *European journal of gastroenterology & hepatology, 9*(3), 299-302.

Trumbach, R. (1993). London's Sapphists: From Three Sexes to Four Genders in the Making of Modern Culture. In G. Herdt (Ed.), *Third Sex Third Gender: Beyond Sexual Dimorphism in Culture and History* (pp. 111-136). New York: Zone Books.

Turrion-Merino, L., Urech-García-de-la-Vega, M., Miguel-Gomez, L., Harto-Castaño, A. & Jaen-Olasolo, P. (2015). Severe acne in female-to-male transgender patients. *JAMA dermatology, 151*(11), 1260-1261.

UK Government. (2017). Change your name by deed poll. Retrieved from https://www.gov.uk/change-name-deed-poll/make-an-adult-deed-poll

UK Trans Info. (2017). Applying for a passport: Additional information for transgender and transsexual customers. Retrieved from https://uktrans.info/legislation/41-name-and-gender-record-changes/62-applying-for-a-passport-additional-information-for-transgender-and-transsexual-customers

Van Borsel, J., Van Eynde, E., De Cuypere, G. & Bonte, K. (2008). Feminine after cricothyroid approximation? *Journal of Voice, 22*(3), 379-384.

Van Der Sluis, W. B., Bouman, M.-B., Buncamper, M. E., Pigot, G. L., Mullender, M. G. & Meijerink, W. J. (2016). Clinical characteristics and management of neovaginal fistulas after vaginoplasty in transgender women. *Obstetrics & Gynecology, 127*(6), 1118-1126.

Van Trotsenburg, M. A. (2009). Gynecological aspects of transgender healthcare. *International Journal of Transgenderism, 11*(4), 238-246.

Vancouver Hospital & Health Sciences Centre. (2002). Transdermal Estrogen Products. Retrieved from http://www.vhpharmsci.com/Newsletters/2002-NEWS/may02nws.pdf

Vanderburgh, R. (2009). Appropriate therapeutic care for families with pre-pubescent transgender/gender dissonant children. *Child & Adolescent Social Work Journal, 26*(2), 135-154.

Vincent, B. W. (2016). *Non-Binary Gender Identity Negotiations: Interactions with Queer Communities and Medical Practice*. (PhD), University of Leeds, Retrieved from http://etheses.whiterose.ac.uk/15956/

Von Krafft-Ebing, R.F. (1965[1886]) *Psychopathia Sexualis: With Special Reference to the Antipathic Sexual Instinct: A Medio-Forensic Study*. New York: Arcade Books.

Vujovic, S., Popovic, S., Sbutega-Milosevic, G., Djordjevic, M. & Gooren, L. (2009). Transsexualism in Serbia: A twenty-year follow-up study. *The Journal of Sexual Medicine, 6*(4), 1018-1023.

Wallien, M. S. & Cohen-Kettenis, P. T. (2008). Psychosexual outcome of gender-dysphoric children. *Journal of the American Academy of Child & Adolescent Psychiatry, 47*(12), 1413-1423.

Walsh, R., Begeer, S. & Krabbendam, L. (2017). *Autistic gender identity differences – Resisting the social schema?* Paper presented at the 2nd bi-annual EPATH conference Contemporary Trans Health in Europe. http://programme.exordo.com/epath2017/delegates/presentation/54/

Washington, S., Bayne, D., Butler, C. & Garcia, M. (2017). 215 Bilateral Orchiectomy For Transgender Patients: An Efficient Surgical Technique That Anticipates Future Vaginoplasty and is Associated with Minimal Morbidity. *The Journal of Sexual Medicine, 14*(2), e91-e92.

Weigert, R., Frison, E., Sessiecq, Q., Al Mutairi, K. & Casoli, V. (2013). Patient satisfaction with breasts and psychosocial, sexual, and physical well-being after breast augmentation in male-to-female transsexuals. *Plastic and reconstructive surgery, 132*(6), 1421-1429.

Weinand, J. D. & Safer, J. D. (2015). Hormone therapy in transgender adults is safe with provider supervision; A review of hormone therapy sequelae for transgender individuals. *Journal of clinical & translational endocrinology, 2*(2), 55-60.

Weyers, S., De Sutter, P., Hoebeke, S., Monstrey, G., Sjoen, G. T., Verstraelen, H. & Gerris, J. (2010). Gynaecological aspects of the treatment and follow-up of transsexual men and women. *Facts, views & vision in ObGyn, 2*(1), 35-54.

Weyers, S., Decaestecker, K., Verstraelen, H., Monstrey, S., T'Sjoen, G., Gerris, J., . . . Villeirs, G. (2009). Clinical and transvaginal sonographic evaluation of the prostate in transsexual women. *Urology, 74*(1), 191-196.

White, B. (1952) *Ex-GI becomes blonde beauty: Operations Transform Bronx Youth*. Daily News. 1st December, 1952. pp. 1, 3, 28.

White, T. & Ettner, R. (2007). Adaptation and adjustment in children of transsexual parents. *European child & adolescent psychiatry, 16*(4), 215-221.

Wierckx, K., Elaut, E., Declercq, E., Heylens, G., De Cuypere, G., Taes, Y. & T'Sjoen, G. (2013). Prevalence of cardiovascular disease and cancer during cross-sex hormone therapy in a large cohort of trans persons: a case-control study. *European journal of endocrinology, 169*(4), 471-478.

Wierckx, K., Van de Peer, F., Verhaeghe, E., Dedecker, D., Van Caenegem, E., Toye, K. & T'Sjoen, G. (2014). Short- and Long-Term Clinical Skin Effects of Testosterone Treatment in Trans Men. *The Journal of Sexual Medicine, 11*(1), 222-229.

Wilson, E. C., Garofalo, R., Harris, R. D., Herrick, A., Martinez, M., Martinez, J. & Adolescent Medicine Trials Network for HIV/AIDS Interventions. (2009). Transgender female youth and sex work: HIV risk and a comparison of life factors related to engagement in sex work. *AIDS and Behavior, 13*(5), 902-913.

Wilson, G. & Rahman, Q. (2005). *Born gay: The psychobiology of sex orientation*. London: Peter Owen Publishers.

Winter, S., Diamond, M., Green, J., Karasic, D., Reed, T., Whittle, S. & Wylie, K. (2016). Transgender people: health at the margins of society. *The Lancet, 388*(10042), 390-400.

Winters, K. (2014). Revisiting Flawed Research Behind the 80% Childhood Gender Dysphoria 'Desistance' Myth. Retrieved from https://gidreform.wordpress.com/author/gidreform/

World Health Organization. (1992). *The ICD-10 Classification of Mental and Behavioural Disorders: Clinical Descriptions and Diagnostic Guidelines*. Geneva: World Health Organisation.

Yang, C. Y., Palmer, A. D., Meltzer, T. R., Murray, K. D. & Cohen, J. I. (2002). Cricothyroid approximation to elevate vocal pitch in male-to-female transsexuals: results of surgery. *Annals of Otology, Rhinology & Laryngology, 111*(6), 477-485.

Yelland, A. (2017). Chest Surgery and Breast Augmentation Surgery. In W. P. Bouman & J. Arcelus (Eds.), *The Transgender Handbook* (pp. 251-264). New York: Nova Science Publishers.

Yeung, H., Chen, S. C., Katz, K. A. & Stoff, B. K. (2016). Prescribing isotretinoin in the United States for transgender individuals: Ethical considerations. *Journal of the American Academy of Dermatology, 75*(3), 648-651.

Zhang, W. R., Garrett, G. L., Arron, S. T. & Garcia, M. M. (2016). Laser hair removal for genital gender affirming surgery. *Translational andrology and urology, 5*(3), 381-387.

zwischengeschlect.org. (2011). Christiane Völling: Hermaphrodite wins damage claim over removal of reproductive organs. Retrieved from http://zwischengeschlecht.org/pages/Hermaphrodite-wins-damage-claim

Subject Index

Author Index